Life
of
Miracles

CHAPLAIN RICK PAETZKE

ISBN 978-1-63961-240-6 (paperback)
ISBN 978-1-63961-241-3 (digital)

Christian Faith Publishing, Inc.
832 Park Avenue
Meadville, PA 16335
www.christianfaithpublishing.com

Printed in the United States of America

PREFACE

I would like to give credit to Jesus Christ and his grace for saving me with his life and showing his love throughout my life with signs and wonders. I would like to give thanks to all my family members who were involved in my life—my brothers and sisters, Carol, Barb, Kathy, and Kurt, and my mom and dad, Frederick and Helen Paetzke. They were with me all my life and witnessed most of these things happening in my life. I would also like to give credit to my cousins and friends. When I mention them in this book, most friends are mentioned by first name only, for their privacy. I also thank the technology for allowing me to have scriptures transferred from Bible tapes.

This book is not based on certain doctrines. I'm not trying to tell people what they should believe or what church they should belong to. I am trying to prove to people that Jesus Christ still exists; he's still alive today, and he did rise again from the dead. He's trying to reach out to many people in the world through us, his children, to let them know that they can be forgiven of all their sins and that God wants to be involved in all our lives, if we would only surrender our wills to his and admit to him that we're sinners lost without him. I'm hoping that through this, if you ever have any questions or things like that, you can seek the body of Christ for answers.

People who really believe that Jesus rose again from the dead and who believe in the new birth experience, I hope you enjoy this story. It's all true, and it's to encourage people to believe that God is real today and that he loves you. I bless everyone who reads this book, and I pray that you pass it on—Jesus's name and the scriptures from Bible Gateway. I would not be a chaplain in prison ministry today without Jesus and without the love and support of my family and friends. This story will prove that God is active in today's world and that God's grace is being poured out on all believers.

> But the gift isn't like the trespass. For if by the trespass of the one the many died, much more did the grace of God, and the gift by the grace of the one man, Jesus Christ, abound to the many. (Romans 5:15 WEB)

> The law came in that the trespass might abound; but where sin abounded, grace abounded more exceedingly. (Romans 5:20)

INTRODUCTION

My heart's desire is for my readers to understand that, without a shadow of doubt, I believe in God the Father, and I believe that Lord Jesus Christ is alive and well in this universe. He has been active with the whole world since the creation of the earth. I have borne witness to the fact that God and angels, good and fallen, are actively working in this world. Yes, a battle between good and evil or light and darkness is very evident in this present world. The Bible says that God is the same yesterday, today, and forever. So it stands to reason that he is still working on reaching lost souls that have died spiritually after the fall of Adam and Eve.

I am one in a million that Jesus has called out of darkness. In my story, I will be using three Bible versions: the American Standard Version (ASV), the World English Bible (WEB), and the King James Version (KJV). These scriptures explain my call by the Lord.

> For I know the thoughts that I think toward you, saith Jehovah, thoughts of peace, and not of evil, to give you hope in your latter end. And ye shall call upon me, and ye shall go and pray unto me, and I will hearken unto you. And ye shall seek me, and find me, when ye shall search for me with all your heart. (Jeremiah 29:11–13 ASV)

> Before I formed thee in the belly, I knew thee, and before thou camest forth out of the

womb I sanctified thee; I have appointed thee a prophet unto the nations. (Jeremiah 1:5)

Among whom you are also called to belong to Jesus Christ. (Romans 1:6 WEB)

"It will be that in the place where it was said to them, 'You are not my people,' there they will be called 'children of the living God.'" (Romans 9:26)

CHAPTER 1

My Birth

First, I am from a family of six siblings, but only five lived long enough to have a life. My brother who was born a year after me died a couple of days after birth because he was a premature infant. So it was Carol, Barbra, Frederick (Rick), Kathy, and Kurt, the youngest.

One day, about three years after Barb was born, my mother and father conceived me. While my mother was pregnant, a month before I was born, Father and Mother were driving down a road, going through an intersection, and a car ran into my mother's car door. The car spun around, and in the process, my mother's head hit the windshield, cracking it, as she was thrown around in the front seat. She had no internal injuries but had some bruises and minor cuts. She was okay on the outside, but not on the inside of her womb. Because of the impact of the two cars, I was physically moved a half turn in her stomach. So on March 18, 1961, at around midnight, I was born, but I was breech born. I came out butt first. So from that day forward, I was marked to be different from any of my siblings.

I seemed to be the oddball of the family, vastly different, a very hyperactive child, and accident-prone, in my opinion. I should have died many times in my life. In the chapters ahead, one incident at a time, I will share how my God's mercy and grace kept me moving forward for his purpose, to fulfill his calling in my life.

Before I move on to Jesus's divine intervention in my life to get me where I am today, I want to give you a brief overview of my family life. My father was a city driver for Milwaukee, Wisconsin. My mother was a good homemaker. My father provided for us kids, and my mother took care of us and the daily cleaning of our home. My parents, at that time, had an old-fashioned way of raising us children. There were no "I love yous" told to us. Parents of that time showed love through action, not words. We always had our necessities met, such as clothing and food, but no physical love was given.

From what I remember, my parents were drinkers. My dad was an alcoholic; he went to the bar after work every day. He and my mother would go to family gatherings or get-togethers, and they always got too intoxicated to drive. My family did not have much use for a religious upbringing, even though we were raised Lutherans. From what I could tell, they were atheist or agnostic in their thinking. So as I grew up, I did not know if there was a God or not. I remember a time when I was talking out loud, looking toward heaven and saying, "God, if you are out there and you're real, please show me. I will live for you if you are." I also wanted to know if we could ever see him while we are here on earth.

From here and from this frame of mind, I will share incidents and life-altering experiences that changed my belief in a supernatural God who is the same yesterday, today, and forever. He's still active today with his creation. Yes, Jesus Christ is alive today through his Holy Spirit in his church, meaning his saints. With the help of angels, he is still making himself known to them who seek him and all who are called out for his purpose and for his will to be done on earth as it is in heaven.

CHAPTER 2

Jesus Reveals Himself

Sometime in the past, in the sixties, I was around five to seven years old. I had a reoccurring dream that I believe had to be a sign that Jesus Christ was helping me find him so that his will would be done in my life as it was planned in heaven. I would ask God to prove to me that he was alive in this world. Why was I born? Why did I get picked on a lot? I remember thinking, *Why doesn't everybody love one another? We came from the same bloodline. Are we not all human beings? How could we have popped out of nothing and into the life that we are in today? Something made us who we are today.* Keep in mind that, at this time, I was not going to any church. No one was telling me about God or Jesus Christ; I had no one talking about religious stuff with me. At that time in my life, I was brought up with an atheist view of life.

When I would take a nap or when I would go to bed for the night, I would close my eyes and go into a deep state of REM sleep. I would find myself walking outside, somewhere in a flat land area with some trees and flowers but mostly grassland. I would always be looking to the pretty blue sky, looking for something. At that time, I did not know why I was looking up. But all of a sudden, I would sense that someone or something was following me and watching me. They were talking to each other about me. The strange thing was, I had no clue why these beings were stalking me. I was terrified because they were getting closer and closer to me. At first, I did not see them, but before I knew it, I saw these hideous demons with big *red* piercing eyes that looked like a lizard's eyes. They also had short horns on their head. I could hear them walking toward me and surrounding me. I told them to leave me alone; I did not want them to take me anywhere. But they still came and grabbed me and walked me over to a stone altar. They made me lie down on it. Then they circled around me, chanting something I did not understand, laughing and grinning, walking around me. They said they were going to kill me, and no one would stop them.

Always, at that instant, I would wake up and sit up and say, "Mom, these evil things in my dreams are trying to hurt me. They said they were going to kill me."

She would say, "It is only a dream, son. It will go away."

So I would believe her that time and go on my way to play, thinking it was over. That same night, they would come after me again. Before they could kill me, I would wake up, and I would run to Mom, telling her about those mean monsters in bed and freaking out about that dream. I told myself, *I do not want that dream anymore*, but it happened again, I would say for about three to four days in a row.

One day, after that scary dream, I ran to my mother and told her, "Demons are still chasing me. What can I do?" Here my mother, with not much faith in God and who never even talked to me about Jesus, told me to tell those demons that Jesus said to them to leave me alone and go away, because I belong to him. So that next night, they came after me again, and I said to them what my mom told me to tell those demons. "I belong to Jesus. You cannot have me or hurt me. Go away." To my surprise, they fled. I had a great sense of love and peace after that, and those dreams stopped. So this dream was a turning point for my life at that time. Also, Jesus Christ was drawing me to him and making his presence known to me. Because of that, something evil was trying to hurt me or, I could say, trying to kill me and keep me from finding out who this God is. I would realize in the time to come. My life would be forever changed for the good of Jesus's call on my life.

My readers, you will understand the reason for all these close calls on my life. If Jesus did not help with these close calls, who did? Am I a superman, or is Jesus helping and having his angels watch over my life? You, the readers, decide. Is it divine intervention, or am I plain lucky? For all my stories, I would feel comfortable taking a lie detector test to back them up.

CHAPTER 3

Close Calls

There were three times that my head was cracked open. Two of the times I got my head injured, I was around eight. It was a typical day; I was running around, playing and pretending I was flying. My mother had a big queen-sized bed with a big box spring. I climbed up on it and started jumping up and down. It was like a trampoline. I was bouncing up above the mattress, laughing away. When my mother heard me playing, jumping and laughing on her bed, she said, "Stop jumping on the bed, before you fall off and hurt yourself." Of course, I would not listen. While I was distracted from where I was jumping, I replied, "I will not fall off." I then bounced headfirst off the left side of the bed, right toward the sharp edge of a lamp table, and I hit the sharp corner edge.

After the impact, I got up, stunned, and felt wetness around my head. Also, my head was tingling. Blood was gushing from the top of my skull. I ran to my mother and screamed, "I am bleeding!" She got my dad, and they rushed me to a hospital, where they sewed up the deep gash on my forehead. The doctor said, "Keep an eye on him for twenty-four hours to make sure he does not have a concussion. And stop him from jumping on the bed. He could have broken his neck." Of course, you are talking about a boy who has ADHD. My parents would call me a super hyper child, always on the go, and a chatterbox by nature. About a year later, I was back in that clinic in Milwaukee, on Howard Avenue. They knew at the clinic that I feared getting my head sewn up. They said it would not hurt; they numbed it. Well, I told myself, *No more getting my head cracked open.*

Little did I know that at about nine or ten years old, I would have a close call on another head injury. Already forgetting about the incident in the bedroom, I was jumping on the bed again, laughing away. It was just like last time, but the warning my mom spoke was reworded: "Stop jumping on the bed, before you crack your head open again." At that point, I remembered what happened. While thinking of getting off the bed, I found myself tripping off in an upward bounce, right into an end table corner, and it smacked me right on my forehead, close to the hairline, where I cracked my head open again. It was gushing bad, so my mother had me hold a towel on my head until my father was home to take me to the clinic on Sixth Street, to keep me from bleeding to death.

One day, I was playing with my best friend Kevin, who lived close to me in the Southlawn housing projects. I got up early that morning, ate breakfast, and said to my mother, "I am going over to Kevin's house to play."

She said, "Okay. Make sure you're home for lunch."

I replied, "I will."

I walked over to my friend's house, and his dad answered the door. "Kevin, Rick here wants to go out and play." Of course, Kevin was out in a heartbeat. I said, "Hey, let us go down by the railroad track and hunt for more grass snakes." We walked about a three-mile distance from my home to get to the railroad tracks. By these tracks, one side had a lot of tall grass and trees and big bushes. Kevin and I would turn over big boards lying on the ground; that was where we would find grass snakes.

Kevin said, "Rick, I think I hear other kids who are playing around here." We could not see them, but I think they could see where we were in the tall brush.

I said, "Kevin, be quiet until they go away. I do not want trouble."

But before I knew it, I heard a swishing sound coming my way, and I felt something big hit my head. I felt light-headed and dizzy. I started to feel a wetness all over my body. I looked down at the ground, and there was a railroad spike lying there with a little blood and hair on it.

My friend started to freak out and said, "Rick, you're bleeding bad!"

I was stunned and said, "Are you sure?" Then I noticed my T-shirt was getting soaked with blood. I started to panic and said, "I need to run to get help." But my mind said, *Do not run. Your blood will pump faster. Hold your head with your hand and walk fast, not run.*

I went to my home, which was one mile or more away. My sister got my mother and father to come home to get me to the emergency clinic again on Howard. They knew I was terrified. The doctors said, "Son, while we fix you up, want to fly to the moon and back?"

I said, "How?"

"We got a space suit just for your size."

I said, "Okay. I do not want to be there long."

Little did I realize that it was a stitching-up space suit, where they strapped my arms and legs down to keep me from moving around. While I was talking to them, I asked them why my helmet had a hole on top of my head. Then I heard this loud humming machine coming toward me, right above my head. It came to my head and applied pressure for a few seconds, and then my open wound was closed.

The thing I want you all to know about is the distance and the time to get to the house and to the clinic, and the amount of blood lost on the way to the doctor. He said I should have bled out before I got to the medical clinic. He said I must have a guardian angel watching over me. Praise God. If it is not your time, you will not die.

CHAPTER 4

Foolish Things

One morning, after I ate breakfast, I told my mother, "I want to go outside and play."

She said, "Okay, but be home before lunch."

"All right. See you later, Mom."

While I was outside, a crazy idea came to me: *Hey, around those railroad tracks are a lot of sand piles. Go over to them and play with the sand.* By the way, that place belonged to a concrete company. The sand piles were all close to big filter bars underground, where the sand would flow into a big mixture. That just happened to be the sand pile I wanted to play in. I looked around the area, and at that time, no one was around the sand traps. So this little nine-year-old boy went to explore the sand piles.

While I was playing, something strange happened. I fell forward into the sand pile headfirst, and my head sunk into the sand. I could not breathe or move, but I kept going downward in the sand mixer. I was really scared, and my feet were kicking in the air above the sand.

Before I was sucked into the sand mixer, a man pulled me out of the sand pile. He set me on my feet and wiped the sand off my face and said, "Boy, are you crazy? Do you have a death wish? Do you not know that you were playing on top of a concrete mixer? You are lucky I saw your feet sticking out of the sand and pulled you out. This is not a playground here. Go home now, before I tell your parents you were playing on private property."

So I ran home to my mother. My mom asked, "Where were you playing? How did you get covered with sand?"

I said, "Mom, I was playing at the sand pit. A man saved me from being sucked into a sand mixer."

She said, "Son, God is working overtime with you. You could have died there. I better never hear of you going there again. They could have called the police on you, and then your father would have been upset with you."

As you can tell, this was another close call on my life where Jesus Christ was still watching over me. All that time, I was still clueless that some higher power was protecting and watching over me. God for sure had plans for my life, but I still did not realize it yet.

CHAPTER 5

Day I Almost Died

Every year, my dad would take me up north to my uncle's cottage to do some fishing. At that time, Uncle Carl and Uncle Don, with his son, were up at the cottage for a week with my dad and me for some fishing. My uncle's cottage up the hill had a long pier on the lake. The pier had one big, fat log that had a fishing line. At nighttime, we would put night crawlers on the hooks, cast them out to the water, and hope to catch big bullheads. This special log always sat at the end of the pier. It was big and had a flat surface, but it was not very stable.

One morning, I went to the pier to fish. I decided to stand on the log while fishing. I cast out my line to fish and would reel it in slowly to attract fish to my bait. Eventually, I had to recast my line again and again. At a certain point, my uncle Don came down and saw me fishing on top of the unstable log, and he said, "Rick, don't stand on the log. I do not want you to fall into the lake and drown."

I said, "Okay, I will not fool around on the log and fall in."

He walked away, and after a short time, I was right back on that stupid log, fishing. Of course, you know what happened next. I jerked my fishing rod back hard and lost my balance and fell right into the deep part of the lake. Guess what? I did not know how to swim, and I panicked. While I was sinking, I kept taking water into my lungs. I desperately tried to get oxygen into my lungs but instead took in more water. After grasping for air and bobbing out of water four times, someone grabbed me out of the water and pull me out of the lake. Of course, I blacked out from lack of oxygen and too much water in my lungs.

From what I figured out when I got older, my uncle Carl, who worked as a detective in the Madison Police Department, was trained in CPR. My uncle and my dad, after they revived me from drowning, dried me off and dressed me in clean clothes and put me in one of the beds up in the cottage. When I woke up later that day, I thought, *One minute I was drowning in the lake, but now how did I get dressed and in this bed?* At that time, I went into the kitchen and said, "Hi, Dad."

He said, "Hi, son. I hope you learned your lesson about playing on the log on the pier."

I said, "Dad, I will not do that ever again."

We never talked about it again.

But I tell you, my readers, if God did not get my uncle's attention to me in the water, bobbing in and out, and have him pull me out, this man would not be telling you his story. Yes, again, Jesus spared my life from ending.

CHAPLAIN RICK PAETZKE

All these things happened while I lived at the housing projects located at Sunbury Court. The location was the Southlawn housing projects. Then my father hired a builder to erect us a house at 7832 W Waterford Avenue, Milwaukee, Wisconsin. This was where Jesus was going to reveal himself to me and start; he knew the direction for my life. I would like to show you, using the Bible, how God sometimes interacts with his called ones.

Jesus said in John 14:15–18 (KJV),

> If ye love me, keep my commandments. And I will pray the Father, and he shall give you another Comforter, that he may abide with you forever; Even the Spirit of truth; whom the world cannot receive, because it seeth him not, neither knoweth him: but ye know him; for he dwelleth with you, and shall be in you. I will not leave you comfortless: I will come to you.

> Let love of the brethren continue. Forget not to show love unto strangers: for thereby some have entertained angels unaware. (Hebrews 13:1–2 ASV)

> Because he hath set his love upon me, therefore will I deliver him: I will set him on high, because he hath known my name. He shall call upon me, and I will answer him; I will be with him in trouble: I will deliver him and honor him. With long life will I satisfy him and show him my salvation. (Psalm 91:14–16 ASV)

God also proved to me that demons exist today, in this life. With these and many more scriptures, I will present to the reader how God is still working in believers' lives today.

CHAPTER 6

Part 1
My New Life

> Because he hath set his love upon me, therefore will I deliver him: I will set him on high, because he hath known my name. He shall call upon me, and I will answer him; I will be with him in trouble: I will deliver him, and honor him. With long life will I satisfy him, And show him my salvation. (Psalm 91:14–16 ASV)

We moved to my dad's new house on Seventy-Eighth and Waterford Avenue, Milwaukee, Wisconsin, around 1970. I was nine years old, still in grade school, and my whole family moved there. My dad and mom still had their problems with drinking too much, but they did at least stay sober enough to provide shelter, food, and clothing for all of us. Of course, if we had medical issues, we would see doctors, but we pretty much had free rein to do whatever we wanted, as long as we all got home before the streetlights came on. My parents had the philosophy that kids were meant to be seen, not heard. My dad still worked long hours at Milwaukee County as a truck driver, mainly as a garbageman. My mother was the typical housewife; she would clean the house, take care of the kids, and of course, make sure we all had three meals a day. My time to do whatever I wanted was there, without the supervision of any adults, so I was not shocked that I got into a lot of close calls in my life.

For some strange reason, a lot of kids would pick on me. I thought, *We are all in the world, and we should love one another.* I wanted everybody to like me. One late spring day, when I was around twelve years old, I thought to myself, *Hey, go to the apartment's play area close to home and play there.* So I told my mother I was going to the play area by the apartment complex, and she said, "Okay, have fun. See you at lunch." I said, "Okay, bye."

I ran toward the play area, and out of the blue, two teenage ladies came up to me and said, "Hey, little boy. Where are you going?"

I thought at that time that maybe I was trespassing or that these older girls wanted to beat me up. So I said, "Please do not hurt me. I just wanted to go play at the play area."

They smiled and said, "No, we want to invite you to our puppet show. We are going to have cookies and juice. Want to come?"

I said, "If you do not hurt me."

They said, "No, we want to tell you about Jesus Christ. What is your name, little boy?"

I said, "Rick."

"Great, Rick," they said. "Here, have a puppet glove." It was one of those gloves that cover each finger. The glove had the faces of kids of different races and the word *Jesus* printed on the fingers. One finger had a *J*, another an *E*, another an *S*, another a *U*, and the last finger an *S*. They said that *J* stands for Jesus, and Jesus loves me and died for all my sins. The *E* stands for him giving all who receive him everlasting life. *S* stands for salvation for all those who believe that he rose from the dead on the third day. *U* stands for the fact that all of us can be saved if we receive him as Lord and Savior. *S* stands for salvation for all who confess their sins to Jesus and believe that all was paid for by him on the cross. Doing all that meant that Jesus would take me to heaven someday.

After they explained the gospel to me, they said, "Let's go to the puppet show now." I said okay, and away we went to a tall brick wall, where there were at least seven kids waiting for the show to start. The two girls already had the puppet show stage set up by an apartment wall so that we could not see the puppeteers.

Before they started the show, they gave all the children their cookies and juice to drink, and they gave us an introduction to the story. It was the Bible story about Elijah and Elisha. What I remember of the story was the part where a chariot of fire came down from heaven, and Elijah stepped into the chariot and was taken by a whirlwind up toward heaven. Before he disappeared, he dropped his mantle by Elisha, and the girls said Elisha got his prayer answered that he would have a double portion of God's Spirit in his life. So God answers prayers.

The girls got up from the stage and said, "Who here wants Jesus Christ to come into their hearts, and believes he is here to save us from our sins?"

At that point, I noticed the strangest thing happen to most of the kids. At the invitation, the kids scattered as though they feared that statement. Only a little girl and I were left. The part I thought was strange was that I really liked these girls, and they were very friendly to me. I wanted to know if God was real in the world and if Jesus would save me from being lost so that I can go to heaven one day. In my mind, it was clear as day that there was an evil presence, and voices spoke to me and said, "Run away. Do not listen to them. These girls are crazy. Do not believe them." I thought in the back of my mind that these were sweet, loving ladies; they did not want to hurt me. I thought to myself, *Where are these bad voices coming from?* When I got older, I realized those voices I heard were demons trying to keep me from inviting Jesus into my soul and body.

As the voices continued in my mind, one of the ladies talked to the young girl, and the other talked to me about accepting Jesus into my heart. I said, "Can I see Jesus?"

She replied, "Yes, you can feel Jesus coming into your life."

I said, "I do not know what to pray."

So she gave me the sinner's prayer to repeat, but before I could start praying, the little girl started to cry. I panicked for a second and asked them, "Did you hit her? Why is she crying?"

They said, "No, we did not hit her. She is feeling the love of Jesus coming into her heart." They said she was happy because Jesus's Holy Spirit had come into her heart.

At that point, the little girl smiled and said, "Jesus loves me. I am so happy. I have Jesus with me." Then she ran home to tell her parents.

So I was left alone to pray with the young lady, and I started repeating the sinner's prayer with my eyes closed. I said, "Jesus, please forgive all my sins that I have done. I believe that you came back from the dead on the third day for all our sins." As I was inviting Jesus to come into my body, both my hands were being pulled up toward heaven. I opened my eyes to see who was pulling them up toward heaven. Guess what? I saw that no one was pulling them upward. So I was a little freaked out and tried to pull them back down. Then the most beautiful, peaceful, and loving voice spoke to me and said, "Let go." Suddenly, I felt no fear, only the fruit of the Holy Spirit times ten. His Spirit fully engulfed my being, and I let go of my hands.

As my hands and will were released, I thought I opened my eyes, but I did not, because when I looked, the girls were gone. I saw nothing but blue sky around me, and I thought I could see a cloud being formed around me. It got larger and larger, before I realized it was Jesus in a white robe above me. I could not make out his face; it was like a bright sun. His being was radiant above me. At that point, I was completely engulfed in this beautiful peace and presence; I did not want to leave. I felt more true love than anyone could ever have imagined in my whole being. I wanted to stay with Jesus and not stay on earth anymore. There was no fear at all. Time seemed to stand still, and I heard a peaceful, loving voice speak to me, saying, "I love you, Rick, and I will be with you forever."

I replied, "Jesus, no one loves me here. Please, can I go to heaven with you? I do not want you to go away."

He replied, "I will never leave you or forsake you. I have work for you to do for me on earth. Someday, I promise to take you home with me."

I replied, "Okay, Jesus. I will stay here for now."

At that point, my hands came down, and my eyes opened, though I thought they were already open. Right there in front of me was the girl, smiling at me. She said, "How do you feel, Rick?"

I said, "Great. I saw Jesus. He said he loves me, and I will be with him in heaven someday." I had great joy that I could not hold back, and I hugged the girl and said, "I want to tell my mom that Jesus loves me, and I know I am going to heaven someday."

Years later, when I was with my mother, she told me that she remembered that encounter I had at twelve years old. She, of course, thought I imagined seeing Jesus Christ. I was twenty-one at the time, when I asked about my encounter with God in my youth.

CHAPTER 6

Part 2
The Miracle Healing

Early one spring day, I was home with my sister Barbra and our mother. I was about nine years old, and I was an explorer of things in our home. I always liked to tinker with things located all over the house. My house had three levels. Upstairs was the top level, and the kitchen and dining room were on the main floor or middle level. Then there was the lower level, the basement, where I liked to hide out—or should I say, hang out to play. I did a lot of stupid things down there, and I would get yelled at by my parents for the crazy things I did.

This one crazy day stands out the most to me. My mother was washing clothes for us kids, and I was bored. I was watching her place clothes in the washing machine. It was an old-fashioned washer with a tight roller system. There was a top roller, and it had a bottom roller that was remarkably close to it. These things would squeeze together any article of clothing put in their grasp. Then it would roll out to the other end the article of clothing, with the water being squeezed out on the other end, back into the washing machine. I watched with amazement how a wet piece of clothing would go in one end, and on the other end, it would be squeezed out mostly dry. My mother would then hang them on the clothesline to finish drying. This contraption was very interesting to me, and I was awestruck at how it operated.

As I watched my mother, she stopped and said, "Son, I am going upstairs to go to the bathroom. I will be back. Whatever you do, do not play with the washing machine, and stay away from these rollers."

"Yeah," I said.

She went upstairs at that point, and the third floor of the house was a long distance from the basement. Now anyone who has or has had kids knows that if you tell a child not to do something, that means to a child, "Yes, I get to test this thing out for myself." Of course, I knew it was wrong, but then I rationalized it. *It cannot be wrong if I am helping my mother out.* Yes, of course, by now you realize what I was about to do.

I walked over to the washing machine and started to take wet clothes out of the water. I placed them in the spinning roller and watched with amazement as the water got squeezed out of the clothes. Before I knew it, I had no more clothes to wring out. At that point, I noticed an oven mitt lying on the floor in front of me. I thought, *Hey, dip this thick glove in the water and let the rollers squeeze out the water.* So I placed the glove by the rollers. The rollers would not grab it because they were too close together, and the cooker's mitt was too fat. I thought I got a great idea. *What I can do is help insert it in the rollers. I know what to do: put the glove on my right hand, push it into the rollers until they grab it, and then pull my hand away from the machine so the glove can be made dry.*

This was an unbelievably bad idea that I planned. As the glove began to go through the rollers, I could not get my hand out fast enough, and the rollers took my whole arm in and started to squeeze it. Did anyone see the cartoons where rollers grab people and they come out flat? If so, you know what was going on in my head. I was terrified and screamed out, "Mommy, help me! The machine is hurting me!" I was pulling back, fighting the rolling action on my arm. One thing about this machine is that the bottom roller spins the whole time, but the top only spins when it is touching the bottom roller. So the bottom roller kept rolling and rubbing on the skin of the bottom of my arm; it kept rubbing off layers of skin as I was fighting the rollers to free myself.

As I was fighting for my life, my sister Barb came down to see what I was screaming about. Here I thought my sister would save me, but no, she freaked out and thought I was going to come out flat too. So now she was screaming for my mother.

Meanwhile, my mother thought there was an intruder in the basement scaring us kids. Sad to say, she had a bad case of diarrhea. But she did not care; she ran down three floors to us kids, yelling, "I am coming! What is wrong?" She could only hear us kids screaming. She finally reached the basement and saw my arm being squeezed by the rollers. She ran over and hit the release button on top of the rollers and gently pulled out my arm. Underneath my arm, my skin had been rubbed off to the bone. My skin at that point was like tissue paper; it was mostly rubbed off.

My mother rushed me to the doctor's office since it was early in the day, and we saw our family physician. When he saw my arm, he was very troubled by it and took my mother outside of the office to talk privately. You know that could not have been good, but he did not want me to freak out over what was in store for me in my future visits with him. He said to my mother, "Helen, you need to put this ointment on his wound three times daily to fight infections until we can get it to heal, so we can do another procedure on his arm." Of course, I had no clue what the next procedure was that needed to be done.

So my mother changed the bandages daily with clean ones and placed the ointment on the infected area of my arm. I asked her, "How long will this ointment need to be applied on my sore, and when will my skin get better?"

She said, "A couple of weeks. Then the doctor will see what happens next." I was not too comfortable with this answer.

One day, the phone rang. It was the doctor on the phone, and he asked how my arm was doing and if there was any more discharge coming out, which would mean that I could have gotten gangrene. If not, we were ready for the next step. My mother asked what it was, and he said a skin graft. Of course, I had no idea what that was. My mother said, "Are you sure that's what is next? Okay, Doctor, I will see you next week for the next checkup."

I had to know what a skin graft was and how it worked. I said, "Mom, what is a skin graft?"

She said, "It is when the doctor takes your arm, and he places it on the side of your body in a sling. It stays connected to your side until new skin can grow back on the sore."

I said, "Where will the skin come from?"

She said, "It will grow on from your side."

I said, "If my skin grows on from my side, how will I keep my arm from staying on my side?"

She said, "A simple procedure is done."

"What is that, Mom?"

"They take medical scissors and cut between the arm and your side and separate the two. Then everything will be done."

I was scared stiff. I said, "No, Mom, I do not want them to cut off my skin from my side."

She said, "I am sorry, son, but unless a miracle happens, there is nothing I can do."

At this point, I ran to my bedroom and cried and started talking to God and Jesus about my arm. I really did not know God, but I prayed and hoped he was out there, listening to my request. I said, "Please do not let me have to go back to the doctor for a skin graft. I believe you are the only one who can heal my skin. Please give me new skin so I do not need the skin graft." In a short time, I felt at peace about my skin problem and fell asleep.

The next week came fast, and my mother said, "It is time to go to the doctor to see what we need to do next."

I said in faith, not realizing what I was saying, "It is okay, Mom. The doctor will not have to do anything, because I asked God for new skin."

My mother said, "Okay, whatever you say. It is time to see the doctor."

After about one hour, the doctor was ready for me to come in. In the patient room, he inspected the wound of my arm and gently peeled off the bandages and gauze on it. As he inspected the arm, his jaw dropped wide open, and he called over to my mother, "Mrs. Paetzke, have you put anything else on your son's arm besides what I gave you?" He asked what happened. He said, "He must have guardian angels watching over him." He then came in the room and said, "Rick, you must have an angel watching over you, because you will not need a skin graft."

I said, "That is good, but why not?"

He said, "You grew back new skin where there was not any around."

At that point, I believed there must be a God.

"No, Doctor. Only the anti-infection ointment you gave me."

He then took my mother into the other room, where they could talk alone, and he told her, "I do not know what happened, but your son will not need a skin graft, because his arm grew three new layers of skin out of nowhere. I could not explain where the new skin came from." Again, it was another miracle that Jesus did in my life.

CHAPTER 7

Drawing Me Nearer

My readers, I want to point some things out to you. It is important to know that God does things according to his will and plan for your lives and mine, at his own schedule. He uses all of life's circumstances that we face to get us where he wants us to be, to bring about his will and our life progress at his time and place, and to get us to use our free will to bring about our full salvation. Some things can happen right away, and others happen in progressive stages to fulfill his will on earth. This is a verse that hints at this.

> Whom will he teach knowledge? and whom will he make to understand the message? them that are weaned from the milk, and drawn from the breasts? For it is precept upon precept, precept upon precept; line upon line, line upon line; here a little, there a little. Nay, but by men of strange lips and with another tongue will he speak to this people; to whom he said, this is the rest, give ye rest to him that is weary; and this is the refreshing: yet they would not hear. Therefore shall the word of Jehovah be unto them precept upon precept, precept upon precept; line upon line, line upon line; here a little, there a little; that

they may go, and fall backward, and be broken,
and snared, and taken. (Isaiah 28:9–13 ASV)

I thank Jesus Christ for shedding his blood on that old rugged cross so that all our sins would be forgiven and remembered no more after we believe in and receive his Spirit and blood into our lives; he purged all our sins. That happened with his death, burial, and resurrection, which he performed about two thousand years ago. *Yes*, admit to him that you are a lost sinner and need his forgiveness. Ask his Holy Spirit to come into your whole being forever; ask him to save your soul from hell, which we all deserve. Listen to what Jesus said here in Revelation 3:18–20 (WEB):

> I counsel you to buy from me gold refined by fire, that you may become rich; and white garments, that you may clothe yourself, and that the shame of your nakedness may not be revealed; and eye salve to anoint your eyes, that you may see. As many as I love, I reprove and chasten. Be zealous therefore, and repent. Behold, I stand at the door and knock. If anyone hears my voice and opens the door, then I will come into him, and will dine with him, and he with me.

> According to the law, nearly everything is cleansed with blood, and apart from shedding of blood there is no remission. (Hebrews 9:22 WEB)

Praise God that he took our punishment on the cross so that we can be saved now and forever. Just receive his blood and Spirit into your heart if you do not want to be spiritually separated from him at death. Apply the blood of Christ to your soul. Remember when Moses told the people to apply the blood of a lamb on their doorposts so the angel of death would pass over their houses. The blood was applied on the right and left of the doorpost and on the top of the door. It was a foreshadowing of the Lamb of God placing his blood on our hearts so we can be spared from spiritual death.

Now on with the story of my life. Sad to say, after that awesome experience with Jesus Christ, I did not start going to church or reading the Bible, Jesus's basic instruction before leaving earth. It's a play on words from the Bible title. I continued as any young man would, but the only difference was that God was slowly guiding and leading me to where he wanted me to be. While my life seemed to be going a certain direction, God would send me things in my life path to steer me to his completed path for his call on my life.

One day, years later, my parents went to visit my grandma. After we reached my dad and mom's house, I asked my mom if I could go to the Whittier grade school to play. She said, "Sure. Come back at lunchtime to eat."

I said, "Okay, see you later."

As I reached the play area, I thought, *What should I do now?* Before I could start anything, a young boy came over to me and said hi. I said hi back. He said, "What is your name?"

I said, "Rick."

He replied, "Rick, my church is holding a revival. It is an outdoor event, a tent revival."

I thought, *No way do I want to go to church.* So in my mind, I was thinking of how I could say no. The words I planned to say were "No, thank you. I am too busy. Maybe next time." But what came out of my mouth instead was "Sure, I would love to go." I wondered where those words came from; they did not come from the thoughts in my brain.

He said, "I will come with my dad to pick you up here at six p.m."

Of course, how do I tell him "no thanks" after I said yes? Of course, I was hoping my parents would say no. I said, "Mom, can I go?" while hoping she would say no so I would not have to go or sound crazy. But reluctantly, I met the boy and his dad at 6:00 p.m. after I got my parents' permission to go to the night church service. They said, "Be sure to have his parents drop you off at home afterward." So before I knew it, I was in a church service, standing close to the back of the church, surrounded by Christians worshipping God.

While I was looking around the crowd, a beautiful but weird thing happened to me. My hands were suddenly pulled up toward heaven, and the same loving, peaceful presence filled my soul with great love. A voice said to me, "I love you, Rick, and you will be with me forever, so do not give up on me. Keep trusting me. I will be your protector." Then my hands came down. After that, I was filled with great joy and peace from God.

After that church service, I went home, and my life continued as before. However, I had a strong feeling that God was watching out for me. Though I still did not know where he was leading me, his great hand was working on my life stage by stage, as you will all find out. This was the beginning of him revealing his perfect will for my life.

CHAPTER 8

─────── ⟨∽⟩ ───────

My Teen Years

Even though Jesus Christ was working in and through my life and slowly revealing his divine plan for my life, these times were somewhat the dark days of my life in general. Yes, Jesus was always protecting me and had angels watching out for me, but Satan and his other fallen spirits were trying their best to keep me busy, doing anything that would keep me from getting to know what God's plan for my life was.

At times, God would send people into my life to ask me or invite me to their church or to join AWANA (approve workman are not ashamed) Club, which was a Christian version of the Boy Scouts. On and off, I went to these gatherings. It did teach me some memory verses about Jesus Christ and his words. I even went to outings with Christians, such as roller-skating and other outdoor activities. During those times, I had an okay time. But for some strange reason, I would be there with these people I did not know well, and I would wonder why I'd think that I should ask them to teach me more about Jesus and who he was, and not just have fun activities going on. I realized later that it was Jesus trying to get me to ask more questions about him and the Bible.

Of course, the evil spirits of this time were doing their best to keep me too busy and distracted to grow in my faith. So for most of my teen years, I hung around a lot with unbelievers and young worldly people. I kept my thoughts mostly to myself. I was a jock and loved sports and karate class. I had friends who liked to do crazy activities. This, of course, was to draw my attention away from God and to get me wrapped up in self-pleasing desires.

My parents pretty much let me do whatever I wanted in those days as long as I kept going to school, did my homework, and came home to eat my three meals a day. On weekends, I would call home and stay overnight with my best friend Gary. These were the times I smoked pot and got high. Part of me knew I was bad, but I wanted to be cool and accepted by my peers. So those high school days were filled with partying and trying my best to meet girls. The weirdest thing was, I went to Bradley Tech, which was at first an all-boys school until tenth grade, then it became a coed school. So I did not meet many girls at this school, because there were maybe twenty-five girls to six hundred boys. The odds were against me. Most of the girls were of African descent. It was not that I did not like them; I thought they would not like a white boyfriend, so I never pursued them for that reason.

In my freshman year of high school, I was still taking city buses to school from Seventy-Eighth and Waterford Street to Third and National in Milwaukee, Wisconsin. One day, in the middle of October, after class was finished, the bell rang for the closing of the day, to signal that people could head home. I leaped out of my chair and ran to my locker, got my books and jacket, then ran as fast as I could toward the bus stop to catch the first bus that would take me home. The bus I had to take was the number 14 bus, and it would come about fifteen minutes after school was out. So that was the reason I would always run to catch the first bus; otherwise, I had to wait another hour for the second bus.

When I ran to the bus stop, I would cross a busy Second Street to reach First Street, and this one time, I did not think about looking both ways before crossing the busy street. I made it three-fourths of the way across, and all of a sudden, I felt the corner of a moving car hit me. I flew up into the air and came crashing down on my back on the asphalt street. The driver of the car that hit me stopped and got out to see if everything was okay. Even though he hit me head-on and knocked me into the air, and even though I slammed my back and hit my head, I stood right up and said, "I am fine. I am sorry I ran into your car, but I cannot talk now. I need to catch my bus home."

As I caught my bus and got on board, the realization of the miracle hit me. Jesus Christ had kept me from getting killed or even hurt badly by that car's impact. The only thing I felt was shaken up by the incident that had just occurred.

CHAPLAIN RICK PAETZKE

CHAPTER 9

The Navy Experience

My life in high school slowly started to fall apart. I lost interest in learning. I could not find an interesting trade to learn. Everything I tried seemed to be nothing I wanted to do for the rest of my life. I still could not find a girlfriend to keep me company. Also, I was still partying with my friend Gary. My life was going nowhere fast. I wanted to have money so I could have fun; also, it might help me with the ladies to have my own job.

I started out working at Ponderosa Steakhouse. It was all right, but I was not making enough money to take care of my car and have enough left to impress a pretty girl. In my junior year of high school, I heard of a job that would pay me exceptionally good money to live on. It was working on heavy-duty equipment trailers that were sold to construction companies. One day, before the last year of school, I thought I would stay on and drop out of school. I told my parents, "I am done with school. I got a full-time job at this construction company, so why finish school?" Of course, they tried to talk me out of it, but it was not going to change my mind. I wish I had talked to my employer first, but you know, I was young and did not think things through.

My employer called me into his office before the school year started, and he said, "Rick, you did a great job here this summer. I hate to see you go."

I stated, "Do not worry, boss. I will work for you full-time. I dropped out of school, so I am staying on with this company."

"Rick, what are you talking about? This was only a seasonal position, and there are rumors that they are going out of business." He let me work for a couple more weeks and then said, "Rick, I wish you had talked to me before you dropped out of school. My boss told me we must lay you off permanently."

Here I was, a high school dropout, and I was turning eighteen that year. Thank the good Lord I was still living at home. I had to think of something fast; my parents were driving me nuts at home. So I decided to join the Navy.

On my birthday, March 18, 1979, I went to the Navy recruiter and said, "How do I get the job with the adventure-included package?"

He said, "How long do you want to be in for?"

I said, "Not too long."

He said, "How about the four-year plan with a trade school included, so you will be locked in a trade?"

I said, "Do you have any shorter enlistment options available to choose from?"

He said, "How about the Delayed Entry Program? It is three years of active service and three years of reserves, but you can only go in as a non-designated fireman."

I said, "What is that?"

He said, "You go to the ship, and they will let you decide what trade you want to train in. Just do the course of the field you want."

I said, "I would like to be a machinist."

He said, "That is good. You will probably start out with the machinist mate department."

He and I had two different interpretations of what that was. He was talking about a sailor who works in a hot engine room. I thought I would be working on machine lathes. So I was in for the shock of my life after boot camp.

He said, "Where would you like to be stationed?"

I said, "Somewhere hot."

He said, "Great. There is a ship stationed at Pearl Harbor in Hawaii."

"Sounds good."

He got my testing and swearing-in completed that day.

I joined the Delayed Entry Program. The day I went to boot camp, I would go see a Brewers game for free, and all the new recruits would get sworn in that day on the baseball diamond before all the Brewers fans. We were the Brewer Company in boot camp. My last day as a free man was June 29, 1979. This was the day of the ball game. Then we would take a bus to Great Lakes Naval Station in Illinois. Sailors called the place Great Mistakes of Chicago.

Before the day of the ball game, my cousin Bob and my best friend Norman took me to Summerfest to listen to great music and drink a lot of beer. I drove to the Summerfest grounds in my car. While we were partying heavily there, we heard the Brits band playing the Beatles' music. We were all singing their songs together.

As I was singing some of the songs, I noticed a beautiful brunette singing the same songs close by, and she kept smiling at me. I was smitten with her smile and looks, and I said, "Bob, I am going to ask this girl to join our party." So this was where a girl named Loretta was introduced into my life.

We talked all night, and after the Summerfest grounds closed, I dropped off my friends first, then took Loretta out to eat and talk more. I asked her how we could stay in touch, because the next day, I was going to the ball game. I said she could have one free Brewers ticket to see me get sworn into the Navy. *If she says yes,* I thought to myself, *she will be my wife, and I will love her forever.* Was I in for a rude awakening? Soon my whole life would come crashing down before my eyes.

The days ahead would be my time in the Navy, wherein I would become like Klinger from *M*A*S*H* to try and get out of service. During boot camp, I kept in touch with my girlfriend by letter, telling her that I was looking forward to finishing boot camp in ninety days. I asked her if she would come to my graduation in the Great Lake naval base. She said okay and that she and my mother would come to my graduation ceremony. They wrote me and said that they would come and get a motel close by for that weekend.

I was looking forward to seeing my girlfriend, and I went to Navy Exchange to buy her a steady ring. When I got my short leave after boot camp, I would come home and tell her, "Let us get married and move to Hawaii, where I will be stationed." Little did I know that after the boot camp ceremony was done, she would be kind of emotionally distant. She liked the ring but would not make any commitment to leave, and I would talk to her more when I got back to Milwaukee, Wisconsin.

Sad to say, the news I would get from her, I would not like. It almost destroyed my life. I had been looking for a girl to love me since I was fourteen; now four years later, I had found one, and she was going to send me the dreaded Dear John letter.

Before my short leave orders came, which would tell me the day I would fly out to Pearl Harbor to meet up with my battleship, USS *Morton, her* letter came, saying that a long-distance relationship would not work for her. I made a last effort to talk to her in person when my leave started at home. When I had gotten situated at my parents' house, I gave Loretta a call to get her address. My readers, this last meeting was not for me to get married, which I wanted, but it was a meeting that God planned. Little did I know that she and her family were born-again Christians, and Jesus was trying to get my attention with what was going to transpire.

When I caught up with my girlfriend, who lived on Capitol Drive in Milwaukee, she said that day was a busy one. I said, "What are you up to today?"

She replied, "My sister is getting married today at my church. Do you want to go with me so we can talk?"

I said, "Sure. I really need to talk to you about us."

We both agreed and went to the church.

The sad thing was, God wanted me to recommit to his call, but I was totally clueless about that purpose. I just wanted to get back with my girlfriend and get her to agree to be my wife. I figured out many years later that because her family members were born-again Christians, they did not want their daughter to be unequally paired with me, since they thought I did not know Jesus Christ. Of course, he knew me, but I was running from him.

This church wedding was the strangest encounter I ever experienced. While I sat next to my girlfriend, the bride and groom were singing love songs about Jesus loving them both and them wanting God's blessing on their marriage and having Christ in their center. The strangest thing started to happen to me; I felt a love so strong in my innermost being that I could not understand at the time. I started to cry uncontrollably for something I did not comprehend at the time. Loretta said, "Rick, why are you crying?"

I said, "I have no clue."

"Rick, you really must like my sister getting married."

I said, "No way, that cannot be it. Men usually do not cry at weddings. I do not even know your sister."

This encounter freaked me and my girlfriend out. She must have thought I was a basket case. I wish I could have realized at the time that it was Jesus trying to get me back on track with his call on my life. I was blind to this because my mind was on getting reconnected with my girlfriend.

After the wedding, we went somewhere to talk that was close to a school playground. I pleaded, without any budging from her, for her to marry me. She finally said, "Rick, it is over. We can never work this out. I am sorry, and here is your ring back."

I snapped at her, saying, "You're such a cruel woman to hurt me like this! You're heartless!" I took the ring I had given her to make us a couple and threw it at the playground by the school. I then walked to my car, and she went into her house.

I was crying as I went around the block of her house, trying to figure out how I could get her back. Believe it or not, I sat outside her parents' home all night, sleeping in my car, trying to figure out how to get her back. They must have thought I was a stalker.

The next morning, she said, "Rick, you cannot sleep outside my house. I will always be your friend forever, so please go home."

I left that morning, not knowing if I would ever see her again.

CHAPTER 10

Navy Life

I returned to my parents' house to finish my short leave before I started my active Navy duty in Pearl Harbor, Hawaii, on a destroyer called USS *Morton*. I remember my last days at home before I flew to my ship. I was a complete basket case. I did not want to talk to anyone. My feelings for my girl were constantly on my mind 24/7. I slipped into a very dark, depressive state of mind; it was a miracle I could do any daily chores. I pretty much ate, drink, and slept most of the time.

I said my goodbyes to my family and went to the airport to catch my flight to paradise, but in my world, it was the beginning of a hellish existence. All I could think of was how I could get out of the Navy contract so I could get my girlfriend back in my life.

First, this story I am writing is meant to give you an idea of how emotionally out of touch I was with the real world. The devil was doing his best to keep me in darkness, so I could not see what God really had planned for me. I cannot tell you everything I did, because it would make this book as thick as a dictionary, just with my Navy life. So I will tell you the highlights of the first year and a half of my Navy life. If you know a character called Klinger in *M*A*S*H*, you will know what I was like in the Navy.

I will give you an idea of what the world would call bad luck. When I reached the airport in Hawaii, I left the plane to go to the baggage claim area and get my seabag, with all my clothes and personal belongings in it. I watched as all the luggage went around in a circle, until all the bags had been picked up by the people from the plane. Guess what? My bag never came around. So I went to the airport people at the information center, saying, "My seabag never came down to the baggage area. What's up with that?" They took a long while to tell me it was on a plane in Milwaukee and in transfer to a California flight. "We have no clue where it is. We are sorry," they said, like that was going to help me feel better. I had to go to my ship with only my uniform on my person. Yes, I was not too thrilled about this. First, my girlfriend dumped me. Now this. I gave my mailing address to the airport so they could contact me when they found it. Guess what? It took three weeks for them to tell me it was flown to Guam, out in the Pacific somewhere. I had to buy new clothes for my personal life and my active-duty life. Was this the great start of my Navy career? Of course not. This was only the beginning.

Three weeks later, I was told my seabag was at the airport to pick up. Guess what now? The ship I was on said the uniforms I had were discontinued and changed to a different type, so all my clothes were useless to me. Does this sound like a happy Navy life?

As my life went on aboard the ship, a lot of crazy things happened. First, I found out that I was not a machinist, but a sailor who would work in a hot engine room. Yes, I was not happy, because I told the Navy recruiter I wanted to be a machinist. So I was now fed up with my Navy career. My exit strategies were in the works in my mind. I said to myself, *Rick, you need to get them to boot you*. I wanted out of this contract, but we all know that in the service you are enlisted in, you cannot just quit, because you are under contract.

So the first thing I did was to always report to sick call. One of the things I said I had was an incurable rash from the hot engine room; I said I needed to get out of the service for this. The Navy said, "Sorry, that will not happen. Here's some cream for your heat rash." The next thing I tried was, I told my department head I needed to go to the medical center for my dizzy spells. I could not keep my mind clear enough to think. So they sent me to Tripler Medical Hospital. I let them shoot blue dye into my bloodstream to see where I could have possible blood clots in my brain. Of course, they found nothing physically wrong with me, so they said it must be in my thoughts only.

Yes, while I was doing my best to get kicked out of the service, I drank and did drugs to deal with my depression. During this time, my ship was getting ready to dry-dock to repair hull damage from the seawater. They had had one month of naval drills out at sea before this. I said to my department head, "I have a bad drinking problem, so can I get help for it?" They said okay and sent me to the Navy dry dock. This, of course, was an in-house treatment for alcoholism, where sailors were put on anti-drinking pills. If you drank while on them, you would get super sick. While I was in rehab for three months, away from my ship, I smoked pot in secret to enjoy getting away from active service.

One day, the devil made me so depressed that I got myself some painkillers and a razor blade so that I could commit suicide. It was because my plan so far to get out of the service was not even close to happening. Late one night, I found a secluded spot away from prying eyes, close to the ocean. Sitting on a dock ledge, I said, "Rick, I cannot handle this life anymore." So I told myself, *Take away this pain and cut your wrist with this razor blade.*

As I got the blade close to my arms to cut it open, the weirdest thing kept happening. Something would throw my hand away from my arm. I tried three times, and the same thing happened. I thought to myself, *Why can't I kill myself right? Okay then, I will take all these pills instead.* As I got the bottle close to my lips so I could swallow them all, again another strange thing happened to me. My arms were fighting to keep me from placing the pills in my mouth. Suddenly, my arm, against my will, dumped them into the ocean. I screamed, "Why can I not even commit suicide? This sucks!" So I gave up and went back to my dry-dock camp. Yes, I kept trying to make up any medical excuse I could think of to get out of the service, but Jesus had other plans. Yes, Jesus was the one who kept me from killing myself.

While I was in dry dock, I got into a crazy science fiction kick. I became a Star Wars fanatic. I was even writing a science fiction story called *The Last Space Shuttle Mission.* I had a Yoda on my hard hat and a Star Wars poster in my living quarters at the base. I was always listening to the Star Wars soundtrack.

One day, while I was listening to my *Empire Strikes Back* tape, I was imagining that I was fighting Darth Vader with a lightsaber (of course, I was using a broomstick). This day was barracks inspection day, when the XO of the ship would come to check for cleanliness. As I turned around to strike down Darth Vader, my XO had just walked into my room, and I just missed hitting him with the broomstick. He shouted, "Sailor, what are you doing?"

I said, "Sorry, sir. I was pretending to kill Darth Vader."

He quickly looked around the room and left without a word after my statement.

The next day, I reported to the daily muster station before the officer in charge gave out orders for the next day. Upon the completion of the instruction for the day, the leading officer said, "Fireman Paetzke, stand fast," after the meeting ended. So all the other sailors left, and I stood alone with the officer of the day. He said, "Fireman Paetzke, you have a pink slip from the XO."

I said, "What is the pink slip about?"

He stated that it was orders from the XO to report to the mental health department of the Navy hospital.

I thought, *Wow, is this my exit plan to get out of the service? They think I am crazy. Think of it: I was fighting a fictional character from a movie.* I told myself, *Before I see the shrink, I need to tell them something out of this world.*

When I reached the psychiatrist's office, I knocked on his door. He said, "Come in."

I said, "I am Fireman Paetzke. I have a pink slip from my XO."

He said, "Have a seat and tell me what you think is wrong."

My problem started with this story. I said, "Sir, I am afraid someone is trying to destroy me or maybe kill me."

He asked who was trying to hurt me.

I said, "Darth Vader talked to me and said, 'Come to planet Endor and join the dark side.' I said, 'I will never join you there, or the dark side.' Darth replied, 'If you do not come with me, I will be forced to kill you!' So I told him I would need more time to decide.

He said to me, 'I give you one month to choose!' Then the spirit of Darth Vader left my room. So, sir, that's my problem. I feel the best place for me to go to escape from Darth Vader is to leave the military and go back to Wisconsin."

Guess what? The shrink sent me to the nut ward to see if I was a danger to myself or others. This was not going as planned.

I was in the waiting room at the hospital, waiting to talk to another shrink. While I waited, I noticed a sailor sitting next to me. I said, "Hi, what is your name?"

No answer.

The nurse at the front desk said, "If I were you, I would not talk to him."

I thought he looked harmless, so I ignored the nurse's advice and said, "Hey, man, what are you reading in the newspaper?"

He slowly lowered the paper and gave me a weird look and brought the paper back up to his face.

Yes, I should have gotten a clue, but no, I said to him a second time, "What are you reading?"

He shot straight up out of his chair, screaming in a bloodcurdling voice, "I am going to kill you!"

Before I knew it, two men in white coats came and grabbed him and put a straitjacket on him and took him to the rubber room, if you know what I mean. The nurse said to me, "I told you not to talk to him." Yes, that man's lights were on, but he was not home.

After this encounter, I had second thoughts about this plan. But before I knew it, I was facing the top shrink. He said, "Is it true that Darth Vader talks to you?"

I replied, "Yes."

"Why do you think that if you go back to Wisconsin, he will not follow you?"

I said, "It's my safe zone."

He said, "We cannot just let you go home with this problem. Your parents might think that the government does not take care of their men."

After a long talk, I concluded that this idea would only get me locked up in the rubber room, so I confessed that this whole Star Wars thing was only in my head. Another idea just bit the dust!

There was a time I saved enough money to fly back home. I decided to go AWOL from the ship. I got a ticket, caught a bus to the airport, and got on a plane home. This was a bad idea. When I got home, my parents asked, "Why are you home? You are not even in the time allowed for leave."

I said, "Dad, I do not like the Navy anymore."

He said, "Son, you cannot run for the rest of your life."

After a long discussion, we both concluded that I had to turn myself in. Of course, that was what I did. I went to the Navy recruiter, and he got me flight orders back to my ship. This took less than a week's time.

I am glad my dad wrote the captain a letter to tell him to go easy on me. He said I was noticeably young and immature for my age. I remember a new sailor that had gotten sent to Ford Island, the brig, and he had come back a totally different man. He was a lifer after that. I did not even recognize this new person. When I stood before my captain at my captain's mast, he said, "Sailor, if your father had not written me a letter, I would have thrown you into prison and thrown away the keys. So I will give you a choice of punishments to pick from. You can go to Ford Island for ninety days or get your GED, with proof of your graduation completed." I was not crazy, so I picked getting my GED. Of course, I still got two weeks' restriction on the ship, but I did finish getting my high school diploma, which, of course, helped me years later. Thank you, Jesus.

Another weird day came, wherein the petty officer in charge asked me to clean out one of the freshwater fill tanks. These tanks were exceptionally large; they held water for the entire crew to drink and shower with. They had a ladder that went inside the tank. There was plenty of room for me to stand inside and clean. I thought, *How can I see inside? It's pitch-dark.* So I found a string of light, which was a cable with big bulbs on the end of it. They were covered with wire mesh over the bulbs, but the copper fittings were differently exposed. Like a dummy, I thought I would put those light cables in the tank with me.

However, they were exceedingly long and heavy. I did not want the cable to fall into the water and to the bottom of the tank; the water in the tank was about knee-high. Guess what I did? Without thinking it through, I used a piece of long wet string to tie it above my head.

While I was cleaning the water tank's sides, I felt a weird chill in the air around me. It was like something was in the tank with me. Before I knew it, a voice said, "Why do you not trust me?"

I looked out of the porthole of the tank and replied, "Who's out there?"

No one answered me, so I shook it off and went back to cleaning the walls. Again, the voice came. "Why do you not believe me?"

I said, "Who's out there? Stop playing games with me."

All of a sudden, the string holding the lights snapped. The live bulbs' wire fell into the water, and I was expecting to be cooked (shocked). But instead, I heard a voice say, "Pick it up."

I said, "No, I do not want to be electrocuted." But before I realized it, my hand slowly went to the wire against my will. I tried to not touch the wire, but my hand kept moving by itself. Before I knew it, I was holding it in my hand. I was shocked that I was not getting electrocuted. I thought, *These lines must be water-resistant.* Like a dummy, I used the same wet string to tie it up again.

A couple of minutes passed, and the voice said, "Trust me and believe." I thought I was going crazy. Then all of a sudden, the wire snapped again and fell into the water again. This time, I could hear a sizzling from the wire and bulbs in the water. The voice spoke again: "Pick it up. You will be okay." I did and then said, "I am done with this tank. I am freaking out."

I later talked to an electrician about the string lights I used in the water tank, and I asked if they were waterproof. He looked stunned and said, "Are you crazy? If they fall into the water while you are in there, you would be a crispy critter."

I was stunned to hear this. I said it happened to me.

He replied, "Yeah, sure, it did. Do you know that there are about 440 direct volts flowing through those wires? I do not have time for your fairy tales." He walked away.

Yes, I believe in divine intervention.

CHAPTER 11

Odd Things

There was a short period that I felt I owed God something for saving my life. The devil knew I was being drawn to the truth about the baptism of the Holy Spirit, so he sent a counterfeit religion for me to follow. This was the time I was a Mormon follower. I had a Bible and a book with the teachings of Joseph Smith and his encounters with angels. Their teaching about us all being gods someday was way out there. While I had some conflicting beliefs in this religion, I decided to reach out to sinners about God.

One day, I went down to Hotel Street in Hawaii, where prostitutes and gay people would hang out. As I was walking down the street, I saw a blond hooker talking to the men walking by, saying, "Anyone want a date today?" That was the phrase they used to ask men if they wanted to pay for sex. I reached her, and she said to me, "Do you want a date, sexy?"

I said, "No thanks, but I have something to say to you."

She said, "What's that?"

"Do you know that what you are doing is going to get you thrown into hell? It's a sin to sleep around with strangers. You are committing adultery and fornication."

She said, "I need the money, so do not worry about me."

I said, "I like you, and I do not want you to go to hell."

She replied, "What else can I do? This is all I know."

I thought for a second, then said, "I will help you. Leave this lifestyle and come with me, and I will marry you. This way, you're married, and I can support you."

She was stunned and said, "Are you crazy? Why would you marry a woman who has slept with hundreds of men!"

"I do not care. At least you would not be sinning anymore."

She said, "That's extremely sweet and nice, but you deserve a better woman than me. So no thanks. I've got to go now. Do not worry about me. This is my choice." And she walked away.

As I stood there, shocked that she did not want to change, I noticed some born-again Christians standing at the corners, talking to people about being born again from above. I went up to them and said hi. They said hi back. I said to them, "I cannot believe these hookers do not want to stop sinning and trust God instead."

They said to me, "So, brother, are you born again?"

I paused for a minute and then said, "Yes, I know God."

"That is not what I asked you. I said, are you born again, like Jesus said in the book of John 3:1–16?"

I said, "All I know is, I believe in God, and that's it."

"So you are not born again. You need this to happen for you to go to heaven and be saved. You are just religious, and that will not save you!"

I was mad. "How dare you tell me I am not saved? I read the Bible. You guys are being fanatical about what you believe," I said, and I walked away from them. My saving those hookers was not in the cards that day. So I took a bus back to base and never tried that again. But what those Christians said hung around in my mind for a long time. Did I really know God or Jesus? Was I lost or not truly following the Messiah? Only time would tell that I was being misled by Satan and his fallen spirits.

Yes, my dear readers, believe it or not, this world is being influenced by two spiritual realms. One is Jesus Christ and his angels and saints; the other is the god of this present age, Satan, and one-third of God's fallen angels and Satan's brainwashed followers. His biggest deception is making people think he is not real. Trust me, after you finish this book, you will see that there is a real spiritual world around us, and Jesus is reaching out for people to be saved from their sins. That's why he died on the cross to pay our sins' debt in full. But we need to receive his gift of the Holy Spirit so we can be born again and saved. This is Jesus talking to them who hear him. He is knocking at your heart now.

> Behold, I stand at the door and knock. If anyone hears my voice and opens the door, then I will come into him, and will dine with him, and he with me. (Revelation 3:20 WEB)

CHAPTER 12

Last Days of Darkness

My time from 1980 to 1981 was wrapped up in science fiction and fantasy. At that part of my life, my ship was in dry dock, being repaired so it would be seaworthy again. I was doing a lot of ship repairing at this time. When I was not on duty, I would be drinking or smoking pot while writing my sci-fi book, *The Last Space Shuttle Mission*.

One day, I had a great idea on how to get out of the Navy. There was a day that I had a Black sailor trying to seduce me while I was asleep. I woke up, and he was doing something with my private area. I said, "What are you doing? I'm not that kind of guy, so stop and leave me alone." He did. I found out my roommate was gay, and he was waiting to be discharged from the service. This, of course, would be my exit strategy that I would use to get out of the service. This was my last resort. This lifestyle disgusted me, but it was my last thing to try.

One morning, I went to the officer in charge of my department and told him my problem. I said, "Sir, can you keep what I am about to tell you a secret? Because my life depends on it."

He said, "Fireman Paetzke, what is your problem?"

I said, "Sir, I am having extraordinarily strong feelings for some sailormen I watch on the ship. There are two sailors I like on the ship. I watch them all the time in the showers, and their bodies really turn me on. I am afraid that if they find out, they will kill me, because I think they are straight. But I cannot fight my feelings, so one day I almost touched them a couple of times in the shower. I think it's best that I get a transfer off this ship for my safety."

His jaw dropped open, and he had a totally shocked look on his face. He said, "How long has this been going on?"

I said, "About six months. What should I do, sir?"

He replied, "Fireman Paetzke, we cannot have you here with those kinds of feelings. The military frowns on those actions. So keep those feeling to yourself, and I will start the process to get you relieved from active duty."

I said, "Okay, sir, I will do my best."

I left his office and closed the door and went to my private dorm room, and I was smiling from ear to ear, thinking, *Yes, I am finally getting out of the hellhole of military service, and I can maybe get my old girlfriend back*. Man, was I in for a big surprise in the months to come. God had other plans for me.

CHAPTER 13

Walking in the Light

My job on the ship about this time was to be a fire watch man. This was a job where you watched over private dock workers who did welding on the ship hull. I would watch them weld and see that any hot flash fire did not start. I would hold a fire extinguisher by my side while they were welding. I just read books to keep myself from being bored.

Before I get into my experiences, I want to remind my readers about two things. One is the time I had my vision of Christ at the age of twelve. Jesus told me that someday I would tell others about him and how he saved me from my sins, and many people would come to Christ because of the testimonies I would give. The second thing is, if you read the Bible, there are at least three times that God called out to a believer by name—two in the Old Testament, one in the New Testament. God called out their names at least twice. It was Samuel and Moses in the Old Testament and Saul (Paul) in the New Testament.

There was a Black born-again Christian who was a welder on my ship. He was a private ship worker in the Navy shipyard. His name was Jeff, and he came up to me at least three times and asked me if I wanted to go to his church or come over to his house for Bible studies. He always had a happy, smiling face when talking to me. He made me feel extremely uncomfortable—him and the "Jesus Saves" on his hard hat. He kept telling me that Jesus loved me and had plans for my life. Of course, I was living in sin, so everything he said made me uncomfortable and uneasy.

I would like you to understand two things about my upbringing. One, my parents never talked about Black people at all. I felt that we left them alone, and they left us alone. So in school, I ignored all colored people altogether. Two, I did not know what to say to one or what my family would think of me. So this genuinely nice Black man made me feel extremely nervous to be around him. I would think to myself, *I wish this Black man would stop talking to me about Jesus and let me get back to reading my sci-fi book.* So I would politely tell him, "No thanks. I will let you know if I change my mind. I've got too much to do. I do not have time for Bible studies or church. Thanks, and no thanks." He was incredibly determined to get through to me; it was as if Jesus was reaching out to me. Three times, he found me on the ship. I would see him coming and want to run away, but I could not leave him, because of my fire watch duty.

As time went by, my life went on as normal. I would get up, do my eight hours of fire watch duty, and then get off my watch and change clothes to go out on liberty, anywhere down by the beachfront to catch a tan. Some time had passed since my encounters with that Christian Black man that I forgot he was ever around, and Jesus had other plans in mind.

After work one day, I told myself, *Rick, go out on the town today and get away from this stupid ship.* I did not realize that this thing that would happen next could only mean that God was calling me. In the military, they only address you by your last name. Even sailors talk to you and call you by your last name. My legal name is Frederick A. Paetzke. My nickname, which only my family called me, was Rick, because my dad's name is Frederick also. To avoid being called by my family members when they wanted my attention, they would call me Rick or Ricky. My dad was called Fritz or Fred if others were around who were not family.

So one late afternoon, I was walking off the ship to the quarterdeck, where the ship had a brow for people to walk off the ship and to the shoreline. As I was walking around the ship's main deck toward the brow, I heard a voice call out to me, saying, "Rick!" I turned around and saw the officer of the deck standing there, and I said, "What do you want, sir?"

He said, "Fireman Paetzke, I did not call you."

As I started to walk away again, I heard my name a second time. "Rick!"

I turned again and, with a little frustration in my voice, said, "Who called my name just now?"

The officer of the deck said, "Paetzke, no one called your name. Just go on your way and get off the ship for your off-duty time."

"Yeah, sure, but I know what I heard. Someone called me. I am not crazy," I said. "Whatever. I am leaving now."

Then the strangest thing happened. I heard that voice a third time: "Go to Jeff."

I thought to myself, *Jeff who?*

The voice said again, "Talk to Jeff."

Suddenly, my head turned to my right, and I saw the Black Christian walking on the pier. I thought, *I do not want to talk to him.*

The voice said, "Talk to Jeff!"

I thought, *Okay*, and ran over to him, shouting, "Jeff! Jeff!"

He replied, "Praise God! What can I do for you?"

I said, "I want to go to your Bible study and your church with you."

He said, "What changed your mind?"

I did not want to tell him that a voice told me, so I said I felt it was time for me to know more about Jesus Christ. I made plans to go to his house for Bible study on Saturday and then go to church on Sunday morning.

First, I was shocked that I was going to a Black man's house. Also, I had no clue what they believed. So on Saturday, before he came to pick me up for the Bible study, I prayed, "Jesus, there are a lot of different teachings and churches in the world, so please help me find a church that you want me to be in and do not let me get deceived by the devil. I want to know the truth that you want me to follow." At this time, I had no clue as to what Jeff believed, but a voice told me to talk to him. It was not a threatening voice, but a loving, peaceful one.

So the next time Jeff met me was Saturday evening, and he picked me up in his car. When I got in the car, the nice brother offered me a new Bible. I said thank you, and we drove to his nice home in Hawaii. He shared a lot of Bible facts with me. He told me about the baptism of the Holy Spirit and water baptism in the name of Jesus Christ for the remission of my sins (Acts 2:38–39). He said that the evidence of the Holy Spirit's presence is if I would speak in other tongues. Yes, he showed me the scriptures throughout the book of Acts and 1 Corinthians chapters 12 through 14 and the last chapter of Mark, where one of the signs that Jesus said believers would do was speak with new tongues.

Of course, that night, after all this Bible teaching, I prayed and said, "Jesus, if this is of God, let me receive it. If it is of the devil, let me not get it and give me the power to leave that church. I believe you will be with me and watch over me on Sunday." Yes, a wonderful experience was awaiting me that Sunday morning at the church called Calvary United Pentecostal Church.

CHAPTER 14

New Beginnings

In the month of October 1981, on an early Sunday morning in Hawaii, my whole life would change. From a carnal man to a spiritual man, I was to be born again. Yes, Jesus said in the third chapter of the book of John that, yes, you must be born again to enter the kingdom of God. Jesus wants us to have our dead body's soul filled with his living Spirit, which we lost after Adam and Eve's fall in the garden. We are all born dead in Adam. In Christ, we are reborn into Christ's life-giving Spirit. There are a lot of scriptures that tell us about our new birth. I will share more scriptures at the end of the story of my life.

Now there was a man of the Pharisees named Nicodemus, a ruler of the Jews. The same came to him by night, and said to him, "Rabbi, we know that you are a teacher come from God, for no one can do these signs that you do, unless God is with him." Jesus answered him, "Most certainly, I tell you, unless one is born anew, he can't see God's Kingdom." Nicodemus said to him, "How can a man be born when he is old? Can he enter a second time into his mother's womb, and be born?" Jesus answered, "Most certainly I tell you, unless one is born of water and spirit, he can't enter into God's Kingdom. That which is born of the flesh is flesh. That which is born of the Spirit is spirit. Don't marvel that I said to you, 'You must be born anew.' The wind blows where it wants to, and you hear its sound, but don't know where it comes from and where it is going. So is everyone who is born of the Spirit." Nicodemus answered him, "How can these things be?" Jesus answered him, "Are you the teacher of Israel, and don't understand these things? Most certainly I tell you, we speak that which we know, and testify of that which we have seen, and you don't receive our witness. If I told you earthly things and you don't believe, how will you believe if I tell you heavenly things? No one has ascended into heaven but he who descended out of heaven, the Son of Man, who is in heaven. As Moses lifted up the serpent in the wilderness, even so must the Son of Man be lifted up, that whoever believes in him should not perish, but have eternal life. For God so loved the world, that he gave his one and only Son, that whoever believes in him should not perish, but have eternal life. For God didn't send his Son into the world to judge the world, but that the world should be saved through him. (John 3:1–17 WEB)

Yes, Jesus was the pole that Moses lifted. He was not literally that pole, but what it stood for. In the Old Testament, the people were dying from very poisonous snake bites. If they looked up at the brazen snake, they would not die. If they refused, they died. So Jesus was lifted on a cross for our sins, and we who have been bitten by our sinful nature can look up for the cure to the problem of sin and can live again. Yes, Jesus wants to heal us from spiritual death. If you refuse his sacrifice in this, you will not live with him after death.

That Sunday morning, I got dressed and met Brother Jeff at the main gate of the base to go to church. He picked me up around 9:15 a.m. I got into the car, in the back seat, and he asked how my day was going. I replied, "Okay. I am a little nervous about this." He reassured me that everything would be all right. "Jesus loves you and only wants what is best for you." He did say that the service we were going to was not like most churches I might have been used to seeing. Basically, it was not like the Catholic or Lutheran churches, which are very laid-back and, in my opinion, very boring churches. Jeff did not say that; I just want to give you an idea of what the church was not like. He said the worshippers are very expressive with praise and their excited love for Jesus Christ. He said, "We worship like they did in Psalm 150, with shouting, praising, singing, and even some dancing before the Lord." Trust me, I had no clue what I was heading into. The way they worship God is in the Bible. One book is Psalm 150 (KJV).

> Praise ye the LORD. Praise God in his sanctuary: praise him in the firmament of his power. Praise him for his mighty acts: praise him according to his excellent greatness. Praise him with the sound of the trumpet: praise him with the psaltery and harp. Praise him with the timbrel and dance: praise him with stringed instruments and organs. Praise him upon the loud cymbals: praise him upon the high-sounding cymbals. Let every thing that hath breath praise the LORD. Praise ye the LORD.

Hallelujah!

With all this information going through my mind in Jeff's car, just before we got to the church parking lot, I said this prayer: *Jesus, I want to live for you, but I do not want to get anything that might not be from God. So if this tongues stuff is from you, I want it. If it is of the devil, you are stronger than him. I do not want it. I just want your Spirit to help me live for you from this day forward. In Jesus's name I pray, amen.*

We reached the parking spot of the church. Brother Jeff, his wife, his two kids, and I got out of the car and headed over to the sanctuary of the church. As we stepped through the first door of the church, there was a room with a lot of chairs scattered around, and I saw some members kneeling by the chairs and praying to Jesus Christ. I asked Jeff, "What is this room for? Is this the church area?"

He said, "No, Brother Rick, this is the prayer room. Do you want to pray before the service starts?"

I said, "Sure. Why not?"

I knelt by a chair and started talking to God, but I noticed that there were people praying there who were speaking other languages I did not know. I asked Jeff, "Do some of these people not know English?"

He replied, "No, Brother Rick. Those people are praying in the Spirit." (In other words, they were speaking in tongues.)

Since I had never witnessed this before, I was a little freaked out and said, "Jeff, I am ready to go to the church sanctuary now." I walked up to the third aisle seat in the middle of the church, at the front of the service area, where I could hear and see the church service with no problem. I remember there was a young serviceman sitting in the front row, talking quietly to God.

Before I knew it, the choir members walked into that area of the church and lined up on a choir platform in front of the worship area, and all started to praise Jesus and God out loud, singing about how loving and great Jesus, the Lord our God, is. They all looked so happy there, singing praise to God. Everyone in the sanctuary was singing to the Lord out loud, with great joy in their voices.

Because I had a Lutheran background, this church service seemed to me a lot more different than what I was used to, so I am not surprised that I thought they were a little crazy! I started to pray quietly to Jesus and said, "God, if these people are of the devil, get me out of here. But if this is from you, do not let me leave, with your Holy Spirit in my life and soul." At this point, a spiritual battle ensued, because two voices started to talk to me. One was extremely negative in its messages, and the other one was very peaceful and loving in the messages I received. At this point of the service, I looked up, and all the choir members who were singing looked like they all were glowing in the background behind their bodies. It was as if each face shone from the glory of God around them, like Moses's had.

The battle for my mind began. First, the evil, negative voice would speak to me, then the peaceful voice would speak to me—of course, in my mind. It started like this. I thought, *Jesus, should I leave this church?*

The first response was *Get out of the church. They are of the devil.*

Right after that voice, I believe it was God saying to me, *Did you ever hear someone sing and love Jesus before? How can someone love Jesus and the devil at the same time?*

That was true. I prayed, *Jesus, you are stronger than the devil. If you want me to leave, tell me, and I will walk out. If you want me to stay and this is from you, I will stay. Do not let me leave until I am right with you.*

While I saw all the people around me singing a love song to Jesus Christ, I noticed that the young person in front of me started to shake and jump around in his seat, shouting out how he really loves Jesus Christ, and he looked so happy praising God that it was hard to understand.

Then the negative voice screamed in my head, saying, *Run and get out of here! They are of the devil!*

At the time, I thought it might be God telling me to go, so I prayed, saying, "Jesus, if this is you, help me. If not, do not let me leave here." I thought, *If God wants me to leave, I can get up and go.* Guess what? Two times, I tried to get up out of the pew area, and something kept me glued to the pew. *Okay, God, I believe you want me to stay and finish the service.*

Before I knew it, Pastor Scott came out and preached about Gideon in the Bible. His way of talking about him was so different from what I was used to. He talked as if he was the Bible character; he was literally acting out the story as if he was there. It blew my mind. He was preaching about faith in action and how we need to talk to and believe God regardless of how we believe and see what

God wants us to do. He said that Jesus would never fail us, no matter what the world around us says.

Before I knew it, Pastor Scott finished his message, and he invited anyone there who needed the Holy Ghost to come to the front of the church, to the altar, to pray and receive the baptism of the Holy Spirit. Then I realized that I could get up out of the pew. Part of me wanted to run out of the service, and part of me wanted to know this true living Christ whose presence was different there in the building. All around us, I could feel the fruits of God's Spirit everywhere.

I prayed, *If you want me to go up front, tell me. If not, I will leave the church.*

I wanted to leave the service, and I walked to the end of the pew and started to exit to my right, which would have me leave the church. But something made me turn left toward the altar, not right toward the exit. So I thought, *Okay, Jesus, I will go to the altar to pray.*

I was going very slowly to the front, and after taking two steps toward the altar, all of a sudden I heard the word *Go* and felt a big push from behind. I almost fell, and I looked behind me and said, "Jeff, don't push me. I am going." Guess what? No one was behind me to push me. I shouted out, "Okay, God, I am going!" and ran up to the altar and went to my knees and prayed. "Jesus, forgive me for all my sins. I believe that you died for me and that you rose again from the dead so we can receive your Holy Spirit and become born again."

One of the brothers said, "If you already repented for your sins and believe that God wants to save you and give you the Holy Spirit, start praising him and thank him for dying for you. Praise him for saving you."

I said, "What should I do?"

"Sing from your heart *hallelujah*, which means 'Praise ye the Lord' in English."

So I started saying "I love you, Jesus" and "Hallelujah" with all my heart. Before I realized it, Jesus filled me with the Holy Spirit, and I started speaking other languages that I did not know. At first, I thought I was mispronouncing the word *hallelujah*, but a brother said, "Brother Rick, you have received the Holy Spirit. You're not speaking wrong. It is the Holy Ghost."

I felt out of this world. I felt so much peace, joy, and happiness, more than anyone could ever imagine. It was the fruit of the Spirit times ten. Also, I felt like I had never ever sinned before; it was as if I had started all over again, fresh, a new creation in Christ. For all those who remember the book of Acts, on the day of Pentecost they were filled with the Holy Spirit, and some of the people around said, "These men are filled with much wine." If anyone knows what a super buzz is like, that's kind of what I was feeling at that point. However, it was not a regular intoxicated feeling, but a sober one, with joy unspeakable and full of glory. I remember feeling light on my feet; I staggered like a drunk man but was as sober as can be.

One of the brothers of the church asked me after my praying and praising God, "Do you want to be baptized tonight?"

I said, "Sure. If it's in the Bible, I will do it."

They said in Acts 2:38–39, "Repent and be baptized every one of you in the name of Jesus Christ for the remission of sins, and you all shall receive the gift of the Holy Spirit, For the promise is to you and to your children, and to all who are afar off, as many as the Lord our God will call." Yes, my friends, all of us today can receive this Spirit and be baptized in Jesus's name today. God is the same today, yesterday, and forever; he never changes. Whatever we do, do all in the name of Jesus Christ, no other name given, whereby in heaven we can be saved.

So I went and changed in the dressing room, put a baptism robe on, and walked to the water baptism tank to be buried with Christ in death and come up a new creature in him and have all my sin washed away. I left the old Rick in the tank and started a new life in Christ.

When I came up out of the water, I said, "Thank you, Jesus, for giving me your Holy Spirit."

Before I knew it, the Lord spoke through me, saying, "This was my word to you when you were a young man, that I would always be with you and that power would come into your life. Many people will be touched and saved through your testimony and the words you speak. The power of God will be with you and will reach many people in your time."

I said, "Brother, did you hear that? God's going to use me to reach the lost for Christ."

Yes, my dear readers, after this day in October 1981, I was a totally changed man. My Navy life after that point was totally different than when it started. As I go on with my story, you will witness things that will blow your mind, and this will happen to you. You tell me if you could never believe in a very real and living God that is still working in this present day. I went back to my ship that night a totally happy man who believed that wherever I went, Jesus was right there with me and in me, through the Holy Spirit in my body.

CHAPTER 15

New Man

Therefore if anyone is in Christ, he is a new creation. The old things have passed away. Behold, all things have become new. (2 Corinthians 5:17)

Afterward he was revealed to the eleven themselves as they sat at the table, and he rebuked them for their unbelief and hardness of heart, because they didn't believe those who had seen him after he had risen. He said to them, "Go into all the world, and preach the Good News to the whole creation. He who believes and is baptized will be saved; but he who disbelieves will be condemned. These signs will accompany those who believe: in my name they will cast out demons; they will speak with new languages; they will take up serpents; and if they drink any deadly thing, it will in no way hurt them; they will lay hands on the sick, and they will recover." (Mark 16:14–18)

For in Christ Jesus neither is circumcision anything, nor uncircumcision, but a new creation. (Galatians 6:15)

There are so many promises the Bible tells us about our fresh new life in Christ that this book would be awfully long on God's Word alone. My story, which Jesus gave me, is to help others know that Jesus is risen and is alive in this world still, calling many who will receive him into their life by faith. Jesus sacrificed himself on the cross so our sin nature dies with him, and we are renewed with his Holy Spirit when we accept him into our hearts. Now all our sins are completely forgiven.

On the first day after my conversion, I woke up with a totally new perspective on life. The first thing I remembered when I woke up was that I needed to talk to Jesus about my day and ask him to help me walk in a way that was worthy of his grace. I loved the fact that all my sin was forgiven and gone for good. In my soul and whole being, I really felt like a new person, like I had never sinned before. It was hard to explain. It was like I had a new slate to fill up with new choices, but this time, Jesus would help me every day to make the right choices. I felt I was not alone; his sweet presence overwhelmed me.

I had so much joy and happiness that anyone would love to have and never want to give it up. This change was out of this world, and I did not want to ever give this up; I wanted the whole world to know that Jesus is real and alive today. When I prayed to him, I knew he was listening to me. He even, from the inside, was teaching me how to pray and how to understand the Bible. When I read the Bible, it became alive to me. The eyes of my soul were open; the Word of God became clear to me. The Holy Spirit was teaching me who we were created for and why we were created for him and how we all began and his divine purpose for mankind's plans. All this and more, Jesus was teaching me in my lifetime.

> I will pray to the Father, and he will give
> you another Counselor, that he may be with you
> forever. (John 14:16)

This was all fulfilled by Jesus Christ. That's why angels are sometimes sent out to help the very elect of God. You will notice that a real spirit war is at work. A battle between good versus evil is always going on in this world, but thanks be to God, who will give everyone victory in Christ Jesus. The gates of hell cannot prevail against his church or body, against the bride of Christ. His will be done on earth as it was finished in heaven. Jesus is the beginning and the end. Satan cannot change the final plan; all will come to pass.

Yes, my dear reader, all this grace and love is offered to you. Accept Jesus's offer for new life and have your sins removed. Accept him by faith today. God will come to you. Whosoever will call on the name of the Lord will be saved. It is your call and choice. Choose life, not death. We are all born dead in this life, spiritually dead. We cannot understand Jesus or the Father until he resurrects our dead spirit and breathes into us his living presence.

Yes, from that first day, I was a new creature. Jesus was renewing me day by day. It's just like an infant when it is born; it does not know much of anything, but in time, it grows up to be a mature man. This is what God intends for you. This change will take you your whole lifetime to understand, as well as what the final plan for your life is. When you see Jesus face to face, all of this will then become clear; you will understand why he did what he did in your lifetime.

The next chapters will be on all that God wants me to share with you, the reader, and how he helped me understand his will for my life. Remember, God has a plan for you.

CHAPTER 16

Miracles in the Navy

The first week of my new life in Christ was totally amazing. Jesus was telling the truth about how the Comforter (his Holy Spirit) would come and how he would be in us. He would guide us in all truth and teach us things about himself through his Word. The biggest plus was that he would help you understand when you are walking in flesh or when you are acting according to your old nature. There was no more walking in old sinful desires; there was no more doing sinful things without him bringing to your remembrance your new Christlike nature. In the Old Testament, God said he would write his laws in our heart. No one would need to teach you about him, because he would now be in you.

> "Behold, the days come," says Yahweh, "that I will make a new covenant with the house of Israel, and with the house of Judah: not according to the covenant that I made with their fathers in the day that I took them by the hand to bring them out of the land of Egypt; which covenant of mine they broke, although I was a husband to them," says Yahweh. "But this is the covenant that I will make with the house of Israel after those days," says Yahweh: "I will put my law in their inward parts, and I will write it in their heart.

> I will be their God, and they shall be my people. They will no longer each teach his neighbor, and every man teach his brother, saying, 'Know Yahweh;' for they will all know me, from their least to their greatest," says Yahweh: "for I will forgive their iniquity, and I will remember their sin no more." (Jeremiah 31:31–34)

So I was in a new life, no longer walking by myself. Christ was with me, and I prayed without ceasing. In other words, I would talk to God throughout the day. Yes, my friends, if you are truly born again, you can talk to God through his Holy Spirit daily, all done through your faith in him. This part of your walk with God is very necessary to grow in your faith in him and in his will for your life.

> Now faith is assurance of things hoped for, proof of things not seen. For by this, the elders obtained testimony. By faith, we understand that the universe has been framed by the word of God, so that what is seen has not been made from things which are visible. By faith, Abel offered to God a more excellent sacrifice than Cain, through which he had testimony given to him that he was righteous, God testifying with respect to his gifts; and through it he, being dead, still speaks. By faith, Enoch was taken away, so that he wouldn't see death, and he was not found, because God translated him. For he has had testimony given to him that before his translation he had been well pleasing to God. Without faith it is impossible to be well pleasing to him, for he who comes to God must believe that he exists, and that he is a rewarder of those who seek him. (Hebrews 11:1–6)

One day, I started talking to Jesus out loud while I was walking in a quiet place, and I said to him, "Jesus, I am looking forward to getting out of the Navy soon so I can tell my loved ones about my new life." I wanted the whole world to know that Jesus is real today and that he has surely risen again from the dead, like the apostles said.

As I was thinking about all I would do when I got out, God interrupted my thoughts and said, "You cannot get out of the military, my son."

I said, "Why not, Lord?"

He said, "Are you a homosexual?"

I said, "No, Lord. You know that I am not one." Then it hit me. I made up that life. "But, Lord, I want to tell my parents about you. If I stay in, how can that happen?"

"You can take a leave."

"Okay, Lord. What do you want me to do then?"

"Tell the Navy the truth."

"Lord, they might get mad at me."

"Tell the truth. It shall set you free."

So I came clean with the Navy and told them the truth that I was not a homosexual at all and that God wanted me to stay in the Navy for him. They were stunned but said, "Okay, Fireman Paetzke. It's all set. You can go back to your active-duty status."

This led me to the first miracle that God performed in my life. After I cleared my mistake on my sexual status, God put it in my heart to take a two-week leave so I could share my changed life with my family and friends. So I got my request form from the ship office to fill out for my leave off the ship. This form would go straight up the chain of command, all the way up to the XO on the ship. It would reach five to six people, from petty officers up to the captain. This was a bad time to ask for leave, but God told me in my mind that I would be approved. The first person all the way to five officers up wrote "Disapproved." My last chance was the XO. That was as high as it could go before it would become law and my leave would be denied. I trusted Jesus and submitted it to the XO. The next day, I was greatly blessed. As I looked at the leave request form, it was all

"Disapproved" until the commander in charge, who had checked "Leave Approved." Thank you, Jesus. He answers prayers.

So I went to the travel agent to book a round-trip flight from Hawaii to Milwaukee, Wisconsin. Here I was, on leave and sitting at the travel agent's office. Everything was going fine until the final step. This step I completely forgot about—giving the money for the tickets to and from Wisconsin. The lady agent came back and said, "You're all set, Mr. Paetzke. All you need to do now is pay $679."

I froze and whispered a prayer. "Jesus, I do not have that much money on me. What was I thinking? Lord, where will I get $679?"

After that short prayer, God put it in my heart to go to the Navy credit union. I told the travel agent that I would be back with the money, trusting that God would provide. Why else would he put it in my heart to leave and get the money? I went to my bank, and I knew I only had $5 in my savings, just enough to keep the account open. I prayed, *Okay, Jesus. It is in your hands. I will believe and trust you.* I finally reached the bank agent in charge of Navy accounts, and I said, "I need to get a loan for airline tickets. Can I get one for $679?"

He looked at the loan records and said, "You still have not finished paying off the old loan, so I am sorry. That cannot happen."

"You sure you cannot try anyway?"

He said, "I do not know what else to say, sir."

I said, "Okay, I will be back."

I went outside to find a private place to pray. With sadness in my prayer, I said, "Jesus, why put it in my heart to take leave? It could have been disapproved, but no, you had the XO approve it. Here I am, on my two-week leave, with no way home. What do you want me to do?"

As I was talking to Jesus about my problem, he spoke to my heart again and said, *Do you trust me and believe, son?*

"Yes, Jesus. I know you can do anything you want. Nothing is impossible for you."

He told me to go back into the bank and get the money I needed.

I said, "Okay, Lord. You know what happened last time, but I will try again."

I finally reached the loan person again, and he said, "Well, Mr. Paetzke, what's your plan?"

I said without thinking, "God told me to get the money from you today, so please check again and see if I can get the loan for my plane tickets."

He typed away on his computer for about ten minutes and said to me, "I'm sorry, Mr. Paetzke, but no loan still." Then he said something very surprising to me. "Sir, why do you want a loan? Just take it out of your savings account."

I almost said that's impossible to do, as I only had $5 in it. As I was thinking this, he said, "Do you want to use that?"

I said, "How much is in my saving account?"

"You have enough for your request, $679."

My jaw dropped, and I said out loud without thinking, "Thank you, Jesus, for providing me the money." With joy, I took out the money and went to the travel agent and paid for the airline tickets. Yes, that day, I went home to Wisconsin to tell my family how God is alive and well today.

CHAPTER 17

Seeing My Parents

I got to the Milwaukee airport around 7:00 p.m. that day, and my uncle picked me up at the airport and dropped me off at my parents' home on Seventy-Eighth and Waterford Avenue in Milwaukee. I was excited to be home. I thought, *Hey, this will be great if my whole family accepts Christ into their hearts*. We all gave each other hugs, and I thanked them for letting me stay with them for my two-week leave. My brother Kurt and my sister Kathy were there with my mom and dad. My two other sisters were already married and living with their new husbands.

When the time came, I witnessed to each family member about my new life in Christ and how being a born-again Christian was an awesome lifestyle because God is real and alive in this present world. I told them how Jesus gave me the baptism of the Spirit in Hawaii, in a Pentecostal church. Some thought it was nice for me, others thought it would not last, and others thought I was in a cult or brainwashed.

It is sad when you tell them the truth of your experience and the devil gets involved and poisons their minds against what you say. We have all come into our bodies and driven out the evil spirit's bondage in our lives before, and our eyes are open; however, the nonbeliever is still in darkness. Flesh and blood cannot understand the Word of God unless Jesus opens up our understanding. God knows when and how he will reveal himself to others when ready. It is said in God's

Word that he has chosen you and called you out of darkness into his marvelous light. If you get a chance, look in the Bible for the parable of the sower and the seed. It will show you what kind of people are out there and how each one receives the truth of the Word of God.

> When a great multitude came together, and people from every city were coming to him, he spoke by a parable. "The farmer went out to sow his seed. As he sowed, some fell along the road, and it was trampled underfoot, and the birds of the sky devoured it. Other seed fell on the rock, and as soon as it grew, it withered away, because it had no moisture. Other fell amid the thorns, and the thorns grew with it, and choked it. Other fell into the good ground, and grew, and produced one hundred times as much fruit." As he said these things, he called out, "He who has ears to hear, let him hear!" Then his disciples asked him, "What does this parable mean?" He said, "To you it is given to know the mysteries of God's Kingdom, but to the rest in parables; that 'seeing they may not see, and hearing they may not understand.' Now the parable is this: The seed is the word of God. Those along the road are those who hear, then the devil comes, and takes away the word from their heart, that they may not believe and be saved. Those on the rock are they who, when they hear, receive the word with joy; but these have no root, who believe for a while, then fall away in time of temptation. That which fell among the thorns, these are those who have heard, and as they go on their way they are choked with cares, riches, and pleasures of life, and bring no fruit to maturity. Those in the good ground, these are those who with an honest and good heart, having heard the word, hold it

tightly, and produce fruit with perseverance. "No one, when he has lit a lamp, covers it with a container, or puts it under a bed; but puts it on a stand, that those who enter in may see the light. For nothing is hidden that will not be revealed; nor anything secret that will not be known and come to light. Be careful therefore how you hear. For whoever has, to him will be given; and whoever doesn't have, from him will be taken away even that which he thinks he has. (Luke 8:4–18 WEB)

I pray that you who read this are on good ground and that you allow Jesus to show you the way to become a true child of God. He is by you now, reading my story. Stop and pray in faith for Jesus to come into your life and forgive you for all your sins, and believe that he died and rose again for your salvation. If you talk to him like you really believe he's there in the room with you, Jesus will come to you and save you.

This is where I will tell you about two people who wanted to believe what I said to them about Christ and who asked me how to be saved and know Christ like me.

My sister Kathy was home one day, and I knocked on her door. She said, "Who is it?"

"It's me, Rick, your brother. Can I talk to you?"

She said, "Sure, come in."

I said, "Kathy, when you die, would you like to go to heaven someday?"

She said, "Sure, but I'm not sure there is a heaven."

I prayed to Jesus in my head, saying, *Jesus, please show my sister you're real so that she can see the light of the gospel.* I told her all about how Jesus came to earth to die for sinners so we all could be made right with God. I gave the short story of Adam and Eve's fall from grace and how God made a way for us to be reconciled to the Father by the blood sacrifice Jesus did for the whole world. I told her that we are all born sinners and that we need to be born again through the

Spirit above. After I explained all this, I said, "Kathy, do you want to receive Jesus into your life now?"

"Yes, but I do not know what to say."

I said, "God will give you the words to say. Repeat after me. Dear Jesus, I believe that you died for my sins, and I am a sinner who wants to be saved from them. I believe that you died and rose from the dead on the third day, and I believe you're here right now in this room."

While she was praying, with her eyes closed, both her arms were raised toward heaven, like what happened to me as a child. As she was finishing the prayer of receiving Christ into her heart in Jesus's name, Kathy asked me why I lifted her hands toward heaven while her eyes were closed.

I said, "It's not me but Jesus who pulled up your hands."

She smiled and said, "Thank you, Rick. Jesus really loves me, and I am going to heaven someday. Thank you, Rick, for telling me about Jesus being real today." She said she was a little shocked that God had pulled her up.

I said, "It's okay. When I was younger, Jesus did that for me also."

From that day forward, God worked in her life. She had more experiences with God but was not highly active. However, later in her life, she came down with cancer, and before she died, she rededicated her life to Christ. In time, she went home peacefully to live with Jesus in heaven. Someday I will see her again. Praise God, this is not the end here on earth.

Later that week, my cousin Mike Paetzke came over to visit. I told him about Jesus Christ also and asked him if he wanted to be saved.

He said, "Sure. What do I say?"

God gave me the same message as before. I told Mike to close his eyes, and we prayed. As we prayed, God raised Mike's hands up also. He said, "Ricky, why are you pulling up my arms?"

I said, "Mike, it's not me. Jesus is pulling you up."

He was also bewildered and said he felt that God loves him. He seemed to blow off what had just happened, and he said, "Thank you for praying for me. I must go now."

I said, "Okay, Mike. I love you. Keep talking to Jesus and read the Bible."

It was not until his later years that Mike became a true, from-the-heart active believer. He now is a brother in Christ. I love him and his whole family.

These are the only two people I recall who had God pulling up their hands. I believe God was showing me that what happened to me at twelve years old was being fulfilled. It would happen to me, as well as my calling to be a soul winner. Christ's power would work through me from those days onward and up until now.

CHAPTER 18

Ministering in Hawaii

When I got back to my ship, I witnessed a lot of strange but true things that happened to me that proved there is always divine intervention being done in our lives by God and even by angels watching over us. Also, God showed me there was a real spiritual world around us, both good and evil.

Yes, demons are real today. There's one thing you figure out as a new believer: that you are a true child of God and have become an enemy of Satan and his fallen angels, who are actively running the course of this world, doing their best to keep people in darkness so that you, the general population, do not come to the light of God's true existence. For sure, the devil will not let you believe he is active in this present world and age.

At first, I wondered why a lot of people who knew me before no longer liked me and felt extremely uncomfortable around me. When the true grace of the Holy Spirit is in and around you, it gets the dark spirits around you stirred up, and people attack you, both physically and spiritually. So in a short span of my growing in Christ, God started to unveil the roots of all the encounters I had with the general public. It was not always people being bad to me; those were evil spirits at work at the time.

I will share some proof that Jesus wanted me to be aware of the fact that, in this existing world, evil spirits do talk through people at times. The first thing I have to tell you is, look it up in the

Bible. Satan is not destroyed yet and will not be locked away until the final judgment. Yes, Satan controls most of the souls that are not saved, but he is limited to those. Those who know that Christ is risen from the dead and that Jesus is set free can be delivered from their own dead nature, with the Holy Spirit in them. Yes, Satan is the god of this present world system, and he runs with certain limits allowed by God, according to God's will and man's free will to serve evil. Therefore, evil is still active in this world. You will notice that Jesus and his disciples cast them out, and until Christ returns, demons are still being cast out. Jesus said to cast out devils in the Great Commission.

By this time in my life, Jesus was showing me that there is an unseen spiritual war going on in this present world, both good and evil, being fought over mankind today. Jesus is trying to save our souls, and Satan is trying to destroy our souls. Basically a battle for our minds' control.

Yes, all this will go on in this world until the return of Christ.

CHAPTER 19

God Intervening

First, I am without a doubt a man who believes that whatever happens to me can only be allowed to happen with God's permission. A fallen evil spirit cannot do anything to you without God's okay, like in Job.

There was a man in the land of Uz, whose name was Job. That man was blameless and upright, and one who feared God, and turned away from evil. There were born to him seven sons and three daughters. His possessions also were seven thousand sheep, three thousand camels, five hundred yoke of oxen, five hundred female donkeys, and a very great household; so that this man was the greatest of all the children of the east. His sons went and held a feast in the house of each one on his birthday; and they sent and called for their three sisters to eat and to drink with them. It was so, when the days of their feasting had run their course, that Job sent and sanctified them, and rose early in the morning, and offered burnt offerings according to the number of them all. For Job said, "It may be that my sons have sinned, and renounced God in their hearts." Job did so continually. Now on the day when God's sons came to present themselves before Yahweh, Satan also came among them. Yahweh said to Satan, "Where have you come from?" Then Satan answered Yahweh, and said, "From going back and forth in the earth, and from walking up and down in it." Yahweh said to Satan, "Have you considered my servant, Job? For there is no one like him in the earth, a blameless and an upright man, one who fears God, and turns away from evil." Then Satan answered Yahweh, and said, "Does Job fear God for nothing? Haven't you made a hedge around him, and around his house, and around all that he has, on every side? You have blessed the work of his hands, and his substance is increased in the land. But stretch out your hand now, and touch all that he has, and he will renounce you to your face." Yahweh said to Satan, "Behold, all that he has is in your power. Only on himself don't stretch out your hand." So, Satan went out from the presence of Yahweh. (Job 1:1–12 WEB)

Yes, I advise you to read the story of Job for how it ended. I believe their power in the name of Jesus. Whatever you do in word or deed, do all in the name of Jesus.

One day, I was walking down the ship's corridors toward the mess deck. I was by myself. A really big, muscular sailor came up to me from behind and tapped my shoulder and said, "Hey, are you the Christian nut I heard about?"

I said, "What do you mean, Jim?"

"I heard that you believe that no one can hurt you, because you are a Christian."

"Yes, that's true. You or anyone cannot hurt me without God's permission. But why would you want to hurt me? I did you no wrong. Also, Jesus loves you, and I love you."

He said, "I do not need your stupid love or your Jesus either."

I said, "Sorry to hear that. I will pray for you."

He said after this, "So you are telling me that if I want to knock you out, God will not let me?"

I said, "Yes. If God does not want you to hurt me, you cannot. Whatever happens is in Christ's control. Sorry, I do not want trouble, and I will pray for you."

I started to turn and walk away from him, but before I had completely turned around, he grabbed me by my shoulder and spun me around to face him. With his right hand, he swung at my face, toward the left side of my lower jaw. I heard a loud smack but only felt a love tap on my jaw. He screamed out in pain, saying, "I think I broke my hand! Your face is like a concrete wall!"

I said, "My face is not that hard. It must be an angel protecting me."

He said, "Man, you're crazy. I am out of here," and stormed out of the mess deck.

Yes, Jesus protected me from harm that day.

CHAPTER 20

More Miracles in the Navy

While I was in my last year and a half of active service, the Lord helped strengthen my faith in my daily life. In this time of my life, I felt God's presence overflowing in my daily life. I talked to him and read the Bible nonstop, and I prayed without ceasing during all my free time. If I was working, I was not thinking about what I was doing job-wise; my mind was on Jesus twenty-four hours a day, seven days a week. I was simply happy to know that Jesus Christ is as real today as he was with the disciples. Some would say I was a fanatic or a Jesus freak, but who cares? I was proud to be a child of God. I believe God can do anything today, as he did in the beginning of the Church Age.

One day, I was walking around my ship, praying to Jesus about finding more souls for his kingdom. I was on the main deck, close to the lifelines that keep sailors from falling overboard. These cable lifelines are made up of twisted strands of hard metal. A lot of them had sharp, razor-like metal strands sticking out of them. These lifelines are not meant to be grabbed or slid around your body. Go figure. That day, without thinking, I grabbed the lifeline and ran my right hand across it. Before I knew it, I had sliced open my palm. It was a deep cut, and it started to bleed. The first thing I said out loud to Jesus was "Help me. What should I do, Lord, to stop the bleeding?"

I heard an inner voice say, *Do you believe I can help you?*

I said, "Yes, Jesus. What do you want me to do? You can do anything."

He spoke to me and said, *Go to the scuttlebutt (a water fountain) and wash it off and believe.*

So I put my cut hand under the water, and as the water ran over the cut, it closed and pretty much disappeared from my hand. I could not show you proof that it was a deep cut. Yes, there was no scar. It was a miracle.

Jesus saved my life from certain death or crippling as I was on duty in the engine room one day. It all started one morning when a fellow shipmate from the engine room department came to my berthing area and told me that my duty was about to start soon. Every sailor had to do different on-duty watches; this was eight hours on and eight hours off. My shift was about to start, so I got myself dressed and headed down the ship corridors toward the engine room. I was partly skipping and singing praises to Jesus Christ, thanking him for another day that I could talk to him and read my precious Bible during my downtime between my walk-through of checking all the engine room gauges. This only took about fifteen minutes, so for forty-five minutes, I would pray or read God's Word until the next hour came up. Now you all know why I was heading to my on-duty station.

As I got closer to the engine room, there was a hatch that was wide open. A crazy thought went through my twenty-year-old brain that said, *Jump into the hatch and onto the ladder that goes down to the engine room.* Let me draw a picture of the open hatch space. It was a solid steel ladder that went three steps straight down and then outward a little bit, so you missed the different engine room valves and engine room pipes that were everywhere. This ladder went about two stories down to the main engine room space. If you fell off that ladder, you could break your neck or other body parts, or worse yet, be impaled on one of the solid steam valves that stuck out all over the engine room. This was not a playground area where you could just not think things through. But this foolish young man did not think that what he was about to do was going to backfire quickly.

I thought it was simple. Jump into the big hatch and right onto the ladder just inside the hatch, and then climb down the ladder to my work space. Simple, right? Wrong. As I jumped into the hatch, I wanted my feet to land on the solid ladder spaces. But as my feet hit the ladder steps, I lost my balance, and instead of grabbing the ladder bars, I started to fall backward, away from the ladder. I cried out, thinking I might die or get badly hurt. I cried out, "Jesus, save me!" As I was falling backward, away from the ladder, after I said "Jesus, save me," I felt something grab me from behind and push me toward the ladder. It made sure that my feet were on the ladder steps, and God or an angel took both my hands and made them grab the ladder with a firm grip. Before I knew it, I was safely on the ladder.

I was stunned for a moment. Then a couple of sailors yelled out from the bottom of the hatch, saying, "Paetzke, how did you get back on the ladder? We thought you were a goner." But before I could say that Jesus saved my life, they said, "Never mind. We know what you will say. Just climb down here before you fall again." I had a nickname already with these men. It was "the captain of the God squad." Yes, my dear readers, God can still save your life today if it is not your time to die. From that point of my life, I found out the power of Jesus's name in dangerous places.

I witnessed to a lot of sailors, and some of them became close brothers in Christ. I want to share two instances that happened while I tried to help unbelievers on my ship. One was Brian, and the other was Stanley.

There is one thing that Christians learn after being saved: you have a great burden for people who do not know Jesus personally. At first, it seems overwhelming. Who should you talk to? What is there to say? How should you say it? And so forth. The thoughts will flow. The best thing that I learned was to trust Jesus to lead you to the people when the time is right. He knows everybody's state of mind and when someone is ready for the Word of God to be planted in their life. Remember, Apostle Paul said, "I plant, and Peter waters it. But it is God who gives the increase." God added to the church who should be saved. We cannot change anyone at all. Only Jesus, in our body, can reach them. So you should study the Bible, meditate, and memorize it, and the Holy Spirit will bring to your mind what you need to say to the unsaved—or even to the saved—to help them get closer to God's place and his will for their life.

Since I did not really know who to talk to, I would sit at an empty table on the mess deck and say, "Jesus, whoever you send to sit by me, I will talk to them and say whatever you want me to say." Other times, I would just walk around and pray, "Lord, if you see me going toward anyone you want to help, have me notice them in front of me, and say 'Talk to so and so.'" Then I would step out in faith and start saying whatever God told me to say. Here are two examples of people I knew nothing about, and this was what Jesus had me say in my encounters with them.

One young man was named Brian. As I was walking around topside of the main deck in front of the ship, I noticed this young man sitting on a hard metal stand, reading a book, and the Holy Spirit talked to my mind and said, *Talk to him about me.* I thought, *Okay, Lord. Give me the words to say.* I said to the man, "Hi there. How are you doing today?"

He replied, "Okay."

I said, "That's good. What is your first name? My first name is Rick."

He replied, "Brian."

I said, "Can I ask you a personal question?"

He said, "Okay."

"Do you believe in God?"

He replied, "No, I am an atheist. There is no god."

I prayed, *Jesus, what should I say now?* Before I knew it, Jesus gave me what to say. I said, "Will you believe in God if I can prove it?"

"How's that?" he replied.

"Just for this one time, I will need you to forget all your preconceived thoughts about God the Father and the Lord Jesus Christ. Have you heard of Jesus Christ before?"

He said yes.

"Okay, just for this moment, I want you to believe that God is real and that Jesus Christ is real and rose from the dead on the third day after being crucified for all sins. John 3:16 said, 'For God so loved the world that he gave his only begotten Son, that whoever believes in him should not perish but shall have eternal life.' Do you believe you are a sinner?"

He said yes.

"If God is real, would you like to be born of God and have eternal life and go to heaven?"

He said yes.

I said, "Then okay. I will never talk to you about Jesus again if nothing happens, but if you feel a change take in your heart, you will go to church with me."

"Okay," he said.

"Say these words with your mouth and believe them for yourself, and God will come into your life. Revelation 3:20 says, 'Behold, I stand at the door and knock. If any hears my voice and opens the door, I will come into him and dine with him, and he with me.' So, Brian, do you want him in?"

He said, "Okay, Rick."

"Repeat these words. Dear Jesus, I believe you died for my sins, and I need you to cleanse me of my sins with your blood and make me a child of God."

As he was saying "Give me your Holy Spirit in my soul," he started to cry and said, "Rick, you're right. Jesus is in my heart, and I feel a great peace and love I've never felt before. Thank you for showing me that Jesus Christ is real. Please take me to church with you."

I said, "No problem, Brother Brian. Welcome to God's family."

He later got baptized in Jesus's name and also got the Holy Spirit's power infused in his life at church. We became awfully close brothers in Christ from that day onward. From what I know, he is still living for Christ today.

Now Stanley was quite a different man when God sent me into his life. This young man had a lot of anger issues he was dealing with. Of course, Jesus at first made sure I did not know these facts. Little did I know that he had been convicted on the ship for many assaults on other sailors. All they did was talk to him, and he punched people out just for that. So I was totally in the dark about his past.

Jesus spoke to me and told me to go to him and say, "Stanley, Jesus wanted me to tell you that he loves you, and he wants to come into your life."

After I said these words, Stanley looked up with a crazy puzzled look on his face and said, "Are you crazy? Do you know who you are talking to?"

I said, "Yes, you're Stanley. Jesus and I love you, and God wants to be your savior."

With a stunned look, he said, "Either you are crazy or you have a death wish or you must know God. You're lucky I did not just punch you in the face, but for some strange reason, I believe you. God really must like me. So I'll let you slide. Please go away now."

I said, "Okay, my friend. If you would like to join Bible study someday, let me know."

He said, "Okay, whatever."

As I was walking away, a sailor came up to me and said, "Paetzke, are you crazy? Do you have a death wish or something?"

I said no.

"Well, it is your lucky day, because no one talks to crazy Stan."

I said, "He seemed nice to me," and I walked away.

Later in the book, I will tell you about how God sent me into his life more and about the supernatural things that happened at his home with some other friends and his wife.

CHAPTER 21

Preparation for Supernatural

The last year and a half of my Navy life was nothing but amazing. The things I experienced were beyond whatever you could imagine or think was ever possible in this time and generation. First, Jesus gave me such strong faith in the unseen spirit world, the world where Jesus's Holy Spirit was always in and working around me all the time. I felt that Jesus was as real as we are in our human form. Whenever I talked to him, I knew he was there, listening and talking in my spirit about things to say or do in my daily life. He showed me a world where demons and angels were real and active in our present world. Remember, God is the same yesterday, today, and forever, and he never changes. Yes, until Christ returns, he will continue reaching out to the world around him to save as many souls as possible with his body, the church.

One typical Sunday morning, I drove to my church in Hawaii and went to the prayer room to pray for God to save more souls in that service and to help me recharge so I could reach more lost souls for his kingdom. I was sitting in the third row of the church pews, in front of the altar. Above that was where the choir would stand and sing, and behind that was the preacher's pulpit. I liked sitting at the front because I wanted to hear whatever God wanted me to hear. I loved praising God a lot; he would give me so much joy in the Holy Ghost. It felt like electricity flowing through my whole being. I would feel so much energy I could run a marathon. I felt pure love and peace and joy unspeakable, full of glory. I was like a battery after dealing with the negative world around me; Jesus would recharge me with his Spirit. That is the living water he spoke about in the book of John.

This special morning, during the worship part of the service, something drew my attention to the back of the church, where the entrance of the worship center was. As I turned my head toward the back of my pew, I noticed three men walk right into the worship center in the back. The strangest thing was, the three men looked like they were in their thirties, which was not bad, but they were dressed like Jesus freaks. Each one was dressed in big robes, with hoods on their heads. Each had sandals on their feet. The one who was in the lead had what looked like a family Bible in his right hand. This book was huge and had a brown leather cover on it.

As they walked toward me, I was thinking, *These guys are very strange people. Are they from some Jesus-freak cult or people who talk about Jesus and do drugs also?* I was thinking that I needed to reach them for Jesus. Before I knew it, the three men entered the pew behind me, and each one lined up behind me—one on my left side, one in the middle, and one on my right side. I said a greeting to them and said, "Thanks for coming to our church service." I reached out to each of them and shook their hands and said, "My name is Brother Rick. What are your names?"

Besides the feeling of the hands, which felt a little odd, not warm but not cold, there was no moisture on them either. It did not feel like a normal hand. *Ah, it is just in my head,* I was thinking, but when they introduced their names, this was the icing on the cake. I kind of blew off their names because I thought they were some cult names. One was Belshazzar, the other Danish, and the other was so crazy-sounding that I blew it off. I was thinking, *These men need you, Jesus. I need to make them feel welcome here.* After our greetings, I asked them, "What brings you to our church?"

Then they floored me and said that God sent them to me to tell me what he was about to do in my life and how he was so proud of my commitment to his kingdom.

I asked them, "How do you know Jesus?"

They said, "We talk to him every day, and he sends us out when he has work to do or a message to get to his called ones."

I said, "Are you his children?"

"Yes."

I was thinking, *These guys are wacky, and they really need Jesus in their life. Here they are, talking to me as if they talk to him face-to-face.* I said, going along with them, "What does God want me to hear from you?"

They opened the book. I could not see the pages; only the brown leather part was facing me. They read from the book like it was a Bible verse addressed to me. "I will be with you in the spirit and will guide your path in the ways of the Lord. I have work for you to do in my name." They said many people would be touched by my testimonies, and his messengers would follow me and protect me from evil. I would see things happen in my life. They would strengthen me in my walk.

I said, "Well, that's great, but will I see you again?"

They said, "If he wills it, you will."

I said, after they told me about my life, "Can you stay and enjoy the service?"

They said, "No, he is calling us now. We must depart."

I said, "Sorry to hear that. I wish you could stay." I was thinking, *They really need the Lord.*

They all smiled at me and said, "May God's peace be upon you always."

Then they all left the pews and went to the main aisle and went toward the back of the church, where the exits were. As all three left through the back door, I thought to myself, *I need to run out there and invite them back to the church again.* So I got up and walked to the back door they had just walked out of five seconds ago, thinking they would be in the parking lot. I would say my final goodbye and invite them back again. The craziest thing was, when I got to the parking lot, I looked all around the lot, and no one was walking away or driving away at all. They completely vanished into thin air. I said, "Man, Rick, you must be dreaming or not thinking right. There's just no way they could get away that fast."

So I went back to the service and finished the whole service, pondering all those things they said to me. After the prayer at the end, I went to my brother in Christ and said, "Jeff, did you see those three hippies in the church for a short time? They sat right behind my pew."

What he said floored me. He said, "What three men? I was wondering who you were talking to in the middle of the service."

I was deeply perplexed by what just happened after that statement, until I read this scripture.

> Let brotherly love continue. Don't forget
> to show hospitality to strangers, for in doing so,
> some have entertained angels without knowing
> it. (Hebrews 13:1–2)

The great thing was, all that they said to me came true. I witnessed a lot of supernatural things I could not explain, unless it was Jesus working in my daily life. All this is only the beginning of his call on my life in Christ.

CHAPTER 22

The Supernatural World

On an incredibly beautiful sunny afternoon, I took a walk to the Navy Exchange in the Pearl Harbor area of the naval base. I found a place to reflect on God's Word and talk to Jesus at the same time. As the time passed, about fifteen minutes went by, and two young ladies walked up to me. One had long brown hair. I think she was Asian. The other girl was a white girl with semi-short blond hair. She did the talking. She said, "Hi, I am Nancy, and this is my friend. We were wondering what you are reading."

I replied, "The New Testament." My curiosity was piqued at that statement. I thought Jesus sent them so I could witness to them. I said, "Are you Christians?"

Nancy replied, "No, but I would like to know more about him."

I said, "Sure, I can tell you why Jesus died for the lost world. Would you like to listen now as to why he died for our sins?"

She replied, "No, we may have to be somewhere soon, but could you come over to my house on Saturday and tell me more?"

I said, "Sure, but I do not know your address."

She asked if I had a piece of paper, and I said no. She then found a business card in her purse and wrote her address on the card.

When she said bye, I said, "What time Saturday?"

"9:00 a.m."

"Okay. Have a blessed day, girls."

Little did I know that it was a big test for me about the unseen spirit world. Little did I know that she had an appointment with a couple of other Christians at about 10:00 a.m. They knew some things I did not know, until Christ opened my eyes to what was really behind this invite.

I got up early Saturday morning and went off the ship to pray at the end of the pier, where I could be alone with Jesus. I talked to God about everything I could think to pray about, besides praising him for saving me and allowing me to be an ambassador for Christ. Of course, my main reason for this morning prayer was Nancy, so she could find Jesus in her heart and become born again, a new child of God. I asked Jesus to have the Holy Spirit give me wisdom on what to teach her from the Word of God. Remember, when Christ was teaching the people of his time, there were a lot of demons cast out also. God was going to show me that, yes, even in our time, demons are still real and in our world today, like back then. Demon possessions still happen in this present day, which I would find out soon.

I reached Nancy's apartment at about 8:55 a.m. that Saturday. I knocked on the door, and in a couple of minutes, she said through the door, "Who's there?"

I said, "Rick Paetzke. I'm here for the Bible study you asked for." Little did I know that she had evil planned that she thought she would bring on me, not knowing that the power of Christ in me was stronger than the demons of this world.

She opened the door, and there she stood. She looked like she had just gotten out of the shower, with a long bathrobe on. I said, "Did I catch you at a bad time, Nancy? Would you like me to come back a little later?"

She replied, "No, it's okay. Have a seat in the front room."

I said, "While I look up some Bible verses to read to you, would you like to go to your room to get dressed?"

She said, "No, it's okay. You start reading the Bible things. I want my hair to dry first, then I can get dressed."

I said okay and nothing more about it. I just thought it was strange that she did not just take care of all that in her private room.

As she was brushing her hair, standing close to the kitchen, I started talking about why Jesus had to die for our sins. As I was reading from the gospels about Jesus going to the cross and shedding his blood for the world's sins, there was a point where I was reading about the blood of Christ, and in a deep voice, she snarled at me, saying, "Stop throwing fireballs at me."

I said, "What? I am not throwing fireballs at you. I am only talking about Jesus's blood that he shed for us."

Again, she said, "Please stop throwing fireballs at me. Read something else. I will be right back. I want to get dressed."

As I was waiting for her, I was a little perplexed about the fireballs statement. Remember, I had never experienced a demon possession before. I was about one year into my faith, maybe less.

That day, I was wearing my "Jesus loves you" shirt, a hand-made shirt with a smiley face and the words "Jesus loves you" on it. Within fifteen minutes, she, for some odd reason, walked out in a very skimpy two-piece bikini. I was stunned for a moment, thinking, *We are talking about the Bible, and she wants to wear a swimsuit?* I just did not pay attention to her closely, to be polite. I thought to myself, *Maybe after the Bible study, she's going to go swimming.*

Again, I said, "Nancy, the blood Jesus shed for you and me is important. It is what washes away and covers our sins for us. This way, Jesus can come into our hearts after we repent of our sins and believe that he rose again on the third day."

The third time I mentioned the blood to her, she screamed, "Stop throwing fireballs at me! I do not like the blood!"

As things started to make sense, the Holy Spirit sent other Christians to the apartment. After the third fireball statement, there was a knock at the door. She asked me if I could check to see who was at the door. There was a man and a woman at the door. I asked, "Are you Christians?"

They replied, "Yes."

I said there was something wrong with her.

They said, "Brother, can you not tell that this woman is into witchcraft? We came to pray for her."

She snapped at them, "Go away! I do not need your cursed prayers!" She began swearing at them.

Before I knew it, they said, "Brother Rick, are you Spirit-filled?" I said, "Yes, I am."

"Then start praying for Nancy. She has a demon in her."

Now a lot of this was beginning to make sense. All three of us walked toward her and asked the demon to come out of her. "In the name of Jesus, we command you to come out." But just as we stated that, her outward appearance changed and looked very sinister. She was foaming at the mouth; her eyes became glassy-looking and dark. When we were praying for her, the voice she spoke with was not human; it was dark and deep, like a man's voice. She would look at my Christian shirt and cuss it out and say, "I hate Jesus Christ!"

We would reply, "We do not care. You need to come out."

They said, "She wants us here."

We said, "No, she belongs to Jesus Christ."

They replied, "We will not come out. She wants us."

I said, "Jesus loves her and wants her free. Come out of her. Nancy, you need to tell us you want Jesus to set you free."

The demon looked at me with his dark, glassy eyes and said, "Rick, if you ever leave Jesus Christ, I will kill you."

I said, "I belong to Jesus, and he will never leave nor forsake me. Also, greater is he that is in me than you demons of the world."

In time, the devil surrendered. Nancy returned to her normal self and asked what happened.

We said, "Demons were attacking you. You need to renounce the witchcraft and give yourself to Christ fully, or they will come back." We got her to say a short acceptable prayer for Christ to come into her heart, but I think she held back some things. I asked her to go to church with me on Sunday, and she agreed.

That next Sunday, she went to church and heard God's Word but was not willing to surrender her life fully to Christ. "Nancy, if you do not change your lifestyle and stop dabbling in the occult, your life will be worse than before. Please," I pleaded with her, "let Jesus have your life, and be free from the bondage of sin and the demons."

As I drove her home, she said, "I will try, Brother Rick. I know you really care for me. I will do what is best for me. Thanks for the ride and church invitation. Maybe I will see you again someday."

From what I could tell, I feel she did not truly give up her old lifestyle. I pray that someday, if it has not happened yet, she will become a true born-again believer in Christ.

Yes, this was not my only encounter with demons. Trust me, my reader, demons are real in this modern-day world. Satan is the god of this present-day world to the unbelievers. Yes, if you are not a child of God, you are a child of the devil. I am not being mean. This is a Bible truth. Jesus said it also in 2 Corinthians 4:4 (WEB).

> In whom the god of this world has blinded the minds of the unbelieving, that the light of the Good News of the glory of Christ, who is the image of God, should not dawn on them.

In the book of Revelation, the Bible talks about the devil being cast out of heaven, and he makes war with saints. It is an ongoing battle until Christ returns. Someday, the antichrist will start a false church and one world government. After the seven-year tribulation, Christ will come back to save the chosen Jewish people for his name's sake. Yes, Satan hates Christians and the true Jewish people of Israel. He will seal 144,000 of the twelve tribes of Israel.

> I saw, and behold, the Lamb standing on Mount Zion, and with him a number, one hundred forty-four thousand, having his name, and the name of his Father, written on their foreheads. I heard a sound from heaven, like the sound of many waters, and like the sound of a great thunder. The sound which I heard was like that of harpists playing on their harps. They sing a new song before the throne, and before the four living creatures and the elders. No one could learn the song except the one hundred forty-four

thousand, those who had been redeemed out of the earth. These are those who were not defiled with women, for they are virgins. These are those who follow the Lamb wherever he goes. These were redeemed by Jesus from among men, the first fruits to God and to the Lamb. (Revelation 14:1–4)

CHAPTER 23

Seeing Stanley

To refresh your memory, there was a young man on the ship who was an angry sailor who, for no reason, would knock your block off just for talking to him. He was the man I talked to about Jesus Christ, and he marveled at the fact that I would talk to him after all the people he had punched out and that I showed no fear. One day, he came to me and said he wanted him and his wife to have a Bible study at his home off base. So one day, I asked Brian and a couple of other sailors interested in the Bible study if they wanted to go with me to Stanley's house.

One Saturday morning, we got up, got dressed, and ate breakfast on the main deck, then we headed out to my car, which was parked on one of the base's general parking spots. We drove out the main gate and headed to the rural highway that led to Stanley's home. As we were driving down a main highway, which was a long straight road, I was talking to all the guys in the car about Christ and the Bible study subject I would cover. I was not a very smart driver, because I constantly kept looking back at the guys in the back seat while talking to them about God. I was not paying attention to what was in front of me as I was driving. I thought, *It will be a straight road for a while. How hard would it be to keep the wheel straight forward?* My brother Brian was in the front seat, and he would tell me if something was not right. I felt sorry for all those guys in the car; they were all thinking, *How can he drive without looking ahead most of the time?*

As I was about a mile and a half down the road, my brother in Christ cried out, "Brother Rick! There is a kid heading on a bike toward us!" The kid was on my left side on the road and was going to cross the road right in front of the car. My speed was about fifty miles per hour. As I heard Brian tell me to watch out for the kid on the 10-speed bike, I turned my head and body to face the front. There, smack-dab in the middle of the car, only about five feet away, was the young teenager. He froze, and all I could do, seeing that there was no way I could not hit this young man, was close my eyes, jam on the brakes, and shout, "Jesus, help me!" At that split second, the car stopped, and I heard nothing but my guys in the car saying, "He's gone."

I said as I opened my eyes, "What do you mean he's gone? He cannot be. I did not hear anything hit the car. Brian, what did you see?"

"I saw the kid right in front of the car. The next second, he was nowhere in sight, whether in front or at the side of the car."

I said, "No way could he be gone."

Then a friend said in the back seat, "My god, how did the young man get behind the car?"

He was parked right in the center of the rear end of my car. I opened the door and said, "Hey, kid, you all right?"

He responded with a freaked-out look on his face, "Yes, I think so."

I said, "How did I miss you?"

He shrugged in disbelief and said, "I cannot explain it." The kid also knew I should have hit him. He said, "I saw the car one moment coming at me, and then in a flash, I was behind your car."

I said, "I'm glad you are all right. I am sorry for almost hitting you. Jesus was watching over you today!"

He replied, "Yeah, okay. I've got to go." And he rode off to where he was going.

My brothers in Christ all witnessed a miracle. We should have hit that kid head-on, but somehow the car or the kid moved right out of the way of that close encounter. Something we could not explain caused one of the things involved to disappear and reappear in a split second. No other things or logic can make sense of it all. I believe only the kid could explain what he saw with his own eyes. Yes, it was either God or an angelic encounter we had just witnessed. Praise God that I did not kill that kid with my bad driving. Trust me, I never drove like that again.

CHAPTER 24

The Bible Study

My first Bible study at Stanley's was a very strange one. When I reached his home with my brothers and reached his front door, I knocked. A couple minutes later, Stanley came to the door. He said, "Hi, Brother Paetzke. Thanks for coming to my home." I said, "No problem, Stan." He introduced his wife to me and my friends. We all said hello.

I said, "Where would you like to have the Bible study?"

"In our study room."

It looked like a small bedroom, with a couple chairs and a bed. We all found a place to sit in the room, and someone sat on the bed. I set up my Bible study chart and was just about to start the lessons. I asked Stan, "Is your wife not joining us?"

"She said she wanted to watch her show."

I said, "It's okay. Maybe next time."

Stan closed the bedroom door, and I said, "Let us pray and ask Jesus to help us with Bible study so the new people can ask and learn about Jesus and who he is. Let the Holy Spirit open their understanding of the scriptures."

As we were praying, we heard a knock at his front door. Stanley said, "Honey, please see who's at the door." His wife said okay. We heard her go to the door, and she talked to someone outside. I could not make out what the person was saying. After about a minute or two, she called out, "Stanley, he wants to talk to you."

I said, "Stanley, go ahead. I can wait till you come back."

I made small talk with the young men about Jesus and the baptism of the Holy Spirit and how God makes you feel so free and new. Stanley talked for about five minutes with the person at the front door; it sounded like he was getting a little flustered with them. He finally shut the door and slowly walked back to the bedroom, where we were waiting, and he opened the door of the room we were in and closed it. I looked up, and he looked as pale as a ghost. I said, "Who was at the front door, if you do not mind me asking?"

This brother had a bad stuttering problem to start with; he could hardly speak fast enough for me to make out what he was saying. With a freaked-out look on his face, he said, "I do not know the man who came to my door. He was wearing a black robe and had a jet-black hood over his head. I also saw him wearing a big pentagram necklace around the neck."

I said, "So what did he want?"

Still stuttering, he said that the man told him not to listen to me or anything I said about God, or he would be sorry. Stanley had replied, "Rick's a good man, and I do not even know you." So he asked him to get lost. Then what Stanley said to me next pretty much floored me. He said, "After I told him to get lost, the man replied, 'You have been warned,' and he vanished into thin air."

That last comment took the cake. I said, "Stan, you do not need to make up weird stories about things to prove God is real. Do you know how crazy that sounds?"

"But, Rick, I know what I saw. I am not making this up."

Suddenly, the Holy Spirit in me told me to be quiet and listen. As Stan finished his last statement, the bedroom door opened by itself slowly; there was no one there to open it. I felt an extremely negative energy in the room. It got cool, like the AC was cranked up, but there was no air conditioner. Then God spoke to my heart and told me, *There is an evil presence in the room.*

I said, "Guys, I know you feel something in the room, so all of you must ask Jesus to protect you all. Plead for the blood of Jesus to protect us from the evil in the room. Evil spirits in the room would like to possess someone if they open themselves up."

So all started saying, "Protect us, Jesus, with your blood." We pleaded for the blood of Christ to protect us. After I saw what the blood of Jesus did to that woman in witchcraft, I knew that the blood of Christ is how we overcome the devil, using the blood of the Lamb of God. I shouted out to the demons to leave the house in the name of Jesus Christ, and we all heard a loud bloodcurdling scream go out of the house.

Suddenly, there was a sweet peace in the air, and the house felt normal again. They said, "Brother Rick, we need Jesus. Can we go to church with you next time? We have no doubt that God and demons are real."

That was one of the most bizarre things I witnessed in Hawaii while I lived for God there.

CHAPTER 25

Lost in Japan

Our ship was on a voyage in the West Pacific to do naval drills and training on self-defense. Of course, our ship would dock or drop anchor by certain ports around the world. One was at a naval base in Sasebo, Japan. One morning, after morning prayer and breakfast, I went to my brother in Christ and asked him if he wanted to go sightseeing in Japan for a day. He said, "That sounds like fun. Where would we go?"

I said, "Leave that to me. I know God is always with me."

But on this day, I did not think any of this through. You will tell by my story that I did not plan this sightseeing trip clearly. I went to downtown Sasebo. I looked all over the place for a travel agency to see what place we could go. I found a train station, and I saw a pretty countryside in Imari, Japan. It was a beautiful countryside close to the ocean, around one hundred miles away from Sasebo.

Of course, when I went to the ticket counter to get train fare to Imari, none of the ticket counters had people who understood English at all. I felt that God was trying to tell me this was not a wise thing to do. But I was bound and determined to see sights in Japan. One ticket agent told me in broken English to call a ticket agency on the phone. So I got a woman who worked for the train station on the phone, who also knew extraordinarily little English, to get me tickets for the train to the village of Imari, Japan. It seemed like it took me a whole hour on the phone just to get the tickets. I was simply happy

I got tickets to go to that countryside, without even knowing all the facts of what I had just purchased at the train station. Here I spent most of Brian's and my money to go to that village. I had only ¥70 left—about $2.75 in American money.

I went back to the ship, found my friend Brian, and said, "I got us tickets to go to a pretty place in Japan." I told him where we were going and said we needed to go to our train bound for that town and be at the train station about an hour before departure. We got to the train station and waited for a short time, and the boarding of the train heading to Imari was announced on the train station speakers; it was to be boarded now. Brian and I got on board the train and found ourselves seats and started making small talk about what we would do and how much time we would spend there in that ocean village. We also talked about things of God while the train traveled long distances and made a couple of stops on the way to Imari.

Brian asked me why we each had only one ticket. "Where is the other ticket for the return trip?"

I was stunned also and said to the train ticket man, "Why are you asking for our ticket? Are you not supposed to stamp it or something?" That was when I figured out I had bought one-way tickets. So with little of our English being understood, I asked the ticket man on the train what time the train went back to Sasebo from Imari.

The train man had a puzzled look on his face, and after a couple of minutes, he said to us, "So sorry," and again, "So sorry."

I said, "Why are you so sorry? What is wrong?"

He then said to us, "This is one-way train. No train go back to Sasebo."

I looked at Brian, and he looked at me, stunned and shocked. He yelled, "Rick, you got us a one-way train to a village with no return plan!"

I said, "I am sorry, Brian. It was hard to get all the information from someone who knows truly little English at all."

He then said, "What are we going to do now, Rick?"

I said, "I do not know. Let me pray." I closed my eyes and prayed, *Jesus, what should I do?* A thought came to me: *Get off at the next stop.* I said, "Brian, we need to get off at the next stop and plan a way back."

He said, "Okay. I hope you know what you are doing."

About fifty miles in the middle of nowhere, the train stopped at a small village. Brian and I got off at a small train station. When we got off the train, the train pulled forward and drove off into the sunset. Here we were, in the middle of nowhere. It was getting late now, and we were totally lost. We both looked at each other and said, "Where are we? This place is very creepy." We were in a country village with maybe a population of twenty-five people. It had dirt paths that led around in circles and snaking twisted roads that passed by little houses like huts. On these trails, there were walled-up areas erected around the village. Inside the enclosure were temples made for the villagers' gods, each one, where people would offer gifts to their gods. It involved money, jewels, trinkets, and anything they thought their gods would like. Some of these places even burnt incense for a little fat Buddha.

As we were walking through the village, with no one in sight, Brian and I were getting a little freaked out, and I said, "Brian, we need to pray to God for help." I said, "Jesus, I made a bad mistake about this trip. I am sorry, God, for this problem we are in. Please, Jesus, help us get back to the naval base in Sasebo, Japan." We knew that if we did not get back in time, the base would report us as AWOL. That would get us sent to captain's mast.

As we were walking down the dirt road, out of nowhere, I saw a little shop or store on the road. I said, "Brian, I will try to get us help to get back to the base. God will help us get back to the ship." Before I went to the shop, I prayed and said, "Jesus, I do not know the Japanese language, so either give me the gift of tongues of their native dialect or anything to communicate with whoever is there in the shop."

I knocked at the shop door, and an elderly Japanese woman came out. I said hi, and she said something in her language and bowed to me. I whispered to Jesus, "How can I talk to her? She does not understand anything I am saying. Can you give me some Japanese languages to speak?" Then God told me to talk to her with charades or paint a mental picture of what I wanted her to understand.

So with her looking at me with a puzzled look and us also feeling lost with our language barrier, I did my best Pictionary thing that God helped me think of. First thing I did was act like I was looking out for something. I acted like I was doing lookout stances. Second, I acted out a battleship firing its canons at something. Then I acted like a lookout person. I said out loud, "Sasebo!" Then I looked to the left, saying, "Sasebo!" Then with the lookout pose, I moved to my right, saying out loud, "Sasebo!" Then I drew a picture of what a boat would look like on the water, using my hands, and said, "Sasebo."

With an excited look on her face, the woman bowed and grabbed my arm and took Brian and me to a paved road for cars to travel on. I thought she would need to know if we had any money for her help, and I told her that I had ¥70 and that's it. She smiled and bowed again.

So here we were, standing by a road. I was thinking, *God, I hope she knows where we need to go, because there are four military bases in Japan and three are naval bases.* We needed to get to the right one, or we would be in big trouble.

With us all feeling awkward, a taxi came down the road, and the old woman waved it down. The driver rolled down the window, and she spoke to him in Japanese. He looked at us, and with an insulted look on his face, he mumbled something in his language to the woman. He just drove away quickly from us.

I said, "Brian, I do not think ¥70 to drive about fifty miles is enough for that driver." I prayed, *Jesus, please get us back to the ship.*

Before I knew it, another car drove up, and it had a young Japanese couple in the front seat. They had purple and yellow and green hair; we could tell by their clothes that they were into punk rock. Their Japanese music sounded like it, but the sound was in Japanese singing. It was very bizarre. The old woman told them some things in their language, but I never heard the word *Sasebo* mentioned.

This nice couple opened their door and invited us into their car, so Brian and I got into the back seat with their loud punk rock music blaring. They started to drive off and waved goodbye to the old woman. We drove for miles, not knowing if they were taking us to the right military base or even to the right place at all. We were driving down long wooded roads and through big tunnels dug out of mountainsides. We were totally clueless about where we were heading.

After driving for hours and over a lot of miles, it was pitch-dark out. They entered a city with some lit areas and then pulled over at a certain entrance by a naval base. With total amazement in our eyes, Brian and I were looking at another entrance to the naval base at Sasebo. Praise God, this was where our ship was docked. God made sure they knew where to take us.

We said our goodbyes to the young couple. They smiled and opened the door of the car, and we got out. I said, "Brian, look, we still have ¥70 left." The couple did not want it. Brian said, "Jesus was definitely looking out for us today." By the way, my brother never went on any more sightseeing tours on train with me again. From then on, it was on foot or by taxi.

Yes, even if you get lost, God can help you get home if you put your trust in him.

CHAPTER 26

Church in Hong Kong

Before I tell you about my ship's travels to the port of Hong Kong, I have noticed that even in small events in life, God can show up in an outward manner to show that he cares about helping you do things for his glory. Yes, even Jesus will do things that do not make sense to human logic, but when our faith is strong and his will is for a certain thing to happen, we see things that will increase our faith and show us that he is active in our everyday lives.

One morning, in Pearl Harbor, before we went on deployment, Jesus helped me see his hands' involvement with two bizarre encounters. One was on a Sunday morning when my brother in Christ David was going to church with me. As David and I got into the Toyota at about 9:15 a.m. to leave the naval base and get to church before 10:00 a.m., I reached over to the key ignition and inserted the key in the slot to start my car. When I turned the key all the way to start the engine, I heard nothing but a short *click, click*. So I restarted and did a second attempt to start my car engine, and it did the same thing twice. *Click, click.* I then spoke to Dave. "The car will not start. It sounds like the starter is messed up. Dave, I know you and I want to go to church bad. I suggest we ask Jesus to help us get to church."

Now that I've gotten older and wiser, I know I should have called for a taxi, but it never crossed my mind. I prayed, *Jesus, there's nothing you cannot do, so please, Father in heaven, help us get to church and back with this so I can praise you and learn about how to be a strong Christian in my daily walk with you.* Just then, as I was asking Jesus to help us get to church, his inner Holy Spirit spoke right into my mind and said, *Turn it on now. It will start.* As I turned the ignition on again, I felt a surge of energy flow through my arm and hand through to the key ignition, and the car fired right up. It sounded like a kitten purring. Nothing was wrong with this car. The first thing David and I did was praise God for helping us get to church. So we went to church, and both of us really felt the joy of the Lord in a great way that day.

I always felt that when I was drained from all the negative energy throughout the week of dealing with the dead world around us, God would seem to give me a recharge of his Holy Spirit for another week of reaching out to the lost world around us. This was God's living water flowing into me from week to week. It was like I was a battery, and God was my charger.

After service was over, we had a short fellowship with the saints of God and went back to the base. Of course, the car started up with no problem, and we drove back to base, to our ship. I left the car in the parking lot until the next day.

When the next day came, I thought to myself, *I will go to downtown Honolulu.* Thinking everything was fine, I hopped into the car, got all ready to drive, and turned the key. Guess what? It would not start again. I got the same *click, click.* I got a mechanic to look it over, and he figured out it was the starter. I said, "Are you sure? Because it started yesterday for me and Dave to go to and come back from church with no problem. Before I drove to church, it clicked a couple of times. We prayed, and it worked fine."

The repairman took out the starter and was totally shocked by what he found. He said, "It is a miracle that you got the car to start at all. To get to church and back with this starter is an impossibility."

I said, "What do you mean?"

"Look at the starter's teeth."

I looked and said, "What teeth?"

"The teeth you need to turn the flywheel for the engine to start. Some of these lose a tooth or two, but this one has no teeth to grab."

So praise God; he got us to church with a busted starter.

Then there was a day when God showed me that there is a spirit war going on all around us every day in our lifetime. I went to see a minister who was preaching in a local town in Hawaii where there was a lot of corruption and evil deeds done daily. Drugs, prostitution, and other vile things happened here in this part of Hotel Street. This was where Brother Parish preached. What I saw there from God's point of view was something I never noticed in the world until now that God's Holy Spirit lives in me.

As the Holy Spirit anointed my brother in Christ, who was preaching to the lost souls in that town, I noticed that some of the locals were not their normal selves. I noticed at least three demon possessions in total operation. One was chatting back in what seemed like backward talking; another person was staring at the preacher with a dark sneer in her voice, and her eyes were black. A third person, a woman, was speaking a weird-sounding language, and between the foreign languages being spoken, she was swearing at him for preaching the Word. They did not like it when he spoke about the blood of Christ.

As I was seeing all this, my new view of an active spirit world was mind-blowing. People who do not have God's Holy Spirit in them do not realize how much demons control people who are not saved. I would not doubt that most of these people Jesus died for are idol worshippers or are involved with the occult or witchcraft.

My dear friends reading this book, if you are not born again of God's Spirit, you will not notice these things. I never did until I was saved from the sinful condition I was in. Yes, my reader, Jesus is calling you to accept him into your life so he can deliver you out of the control of the god of this world. Yes, Satan and his demons are working in the children of the disobedient. Yes, we have all belonged to the devil since Adam and Eve failed God in the beginning. After they ate the fruit of knowledge of good and evil, mankind became corrupt and died spiritually in this world. We all are born spiritually dead; that's why we do not live forever anymore in this world. We need God to put his eternal Spirit back into our lives if we ever want to understand God at all and to be ready to be with him forever after our life here is over. I will talk more about these things as I tell you about my life, with God's divine protection being active all my life.

Let me tell you about something that happened in Hong Kong. I had a church directory of missionaries around the globe, so when we reached Hong Kong, I looked up the church closest to my ship's dock area. I found a Pentecostal church taught by a Brother Curtis. Whenever I had a chance at a port to find a church, I would attend, because I wanted to be around God's people. It felt good to worship and praise Jesus Christ for my salvation. Always, when I went to church, it was like I was a battery, and the negative world drained my positive way of life in Christ. Hearing God's Word brought newness of life to my spirit. The Holy Spirit would fill me with more living water, which would overflow, so when I went back to my ship, I could minister to the lost sailors on my ship.

Whenever I was in a church service, the Holy Spirit would sometimes send electricity through my being. It was not a painful feeling, but a great energy—joy, love, peace, and all the fruits of the Spirit. At times, I had so much of a charge I would either run or jump just to release some of the energy of Jesus's love for me, and my praising him made him happy. The Bible said that God inhabits his people's praise.

Well, this one Sunday in Hong Kong, my brother and I just had a great worship service there, and after some fellowship, we headed back to our ship. I have learned since I've been walking with Jesus that he is always our protector from dangers that Satan may send our way. Sometimes God allows danger to come our way, or like sheep, we wander to places we should not have ventured to. This one day, I must have drunk a lot of fluids. As we were walking back to the ship, which was a couple miles away, I had to go number one bad. This was when God protected me from either death or a bad beating by a foreign people that, when I got older, I perceived were Chinese Communist people. My ship had told us to stay away from any place that stated "No Americans" or, like in Hong Kong, "Chinese only," because sailors would get beaten or killed in those places for no other reason than that they were Americans.

Without looking up to see what this place of business was, I told my companion I would use the bathroom in this business establishment. So he waited outside while I ventured into this establishment, not knowing until I had walked into the place that it was either a bar or hangout for Communist people. I tried to talk to them about using their restroom to relieve myself, but no matter what I tried to communicate to this big group of thugs, it only got them terribly angry.

Suddenly, I felt an evil presence at work in this bar-type atmosphere. The Holy Spirit in me told me to leave now. A man brandished a sword and swung it around a bit, and he started toward me. I turned around and, talking to Jesus at the same time, said, "Jesus, save me from these evil men." I quickly got out of the bad place of business.

When I got outside, the Lord somehow kept them from coming out after me. My brother in Christ said, "Brother Rick, did you not read the sign that said 'Chinese only' on top?"

I said, "No, I wish I had noticed that."

So I found a place to go to the bathroom, and we headed toward our ship. Both of us were thankful we did not get mugged or killed. My faith in God, which was protecting me, was so strong that it was not until years later that I realized all the danger God saved me from.

Yes, my dear reader, if you are a follower of Jesus Christ and are born again from above, just like Job, Satan needs permission to do anything to you. Jesus said, "Greater is he who is in you than he who is in the world."

CHAPTER 27

Part 1
Life after Active Duty

This will be a two-part chapter. First, I will explain why I made some bad choices and how God's grace covered that part of my life. Part one of chapter 27 will be about me starting my life after active duty in the Navy.

To start my explanation of how and why I made bad choices, it's due to the fact that all Christians have a dual nature—the flesh and its human desires, and the Holy Spirit's nature, given to us by Jesus. One wants to please its selfish desires, and the other wants to please God and walk in the Spirit of holiness, in which we have the fruit of the Spirit working in and through us. If we want steady joy in our daily walk, we need to put the word *joy* into three parts. One, *J* is for Jesus first in our daily choices; two, others are second in our daily choices; and third is yourself and your desires. Think of it as this: God's way is to be concerned about what pleases the Father of heaven and his will. Second is to be concerned about how you can help others with the grace of God through you. The third is to put to death the works of the flesh and to try to maintain goals 1 and 2.

I hope by this time in my story, you see why it's so important for God to baptize you with his Holy Spirit, this kill off the carnal nature control over your life, and he makes you alive in your spirit with the power of his presence. Before Jesus comes into our beings, we are dead spiritually. Jesus revives our dead spirit and give us his living Spirit in our body. Now that we have his Spirit in us, we can overcome the fleshly desire that used to rule us, and now we want to walk in his presence daily. Also we can now understand this more every day: the more you pray and read God's Word, the stronger you become.

Our nature, before Christ comes into our being, is the fallen nature that came from Adam and Eve after they ate the forbidden fruit. They died spiritually that day. We all are born spiritually dead to God; that's why we do not seek God or even know of his active presence moving throughout the world. At our birth to our parents, we are all born in sin. We only want to please our own desires and do whatever makes us happy first—the other way around of joy. We are the first person to please. Second, we use others to satisfy our wants and desires. Third, we only want God if we need to be bailed out of a problem or if we want to satisfy our fleshly wants in life.

The devil wants us to be like God and to answer to no one. We think we can keep all of God's rules without his help. So we try and try to keep the law of God and show him we are good enough for him, and at the same time, we only think of ourselves and what makes us happy. But God uses the law of Moses to show us that we cannot ever keep the law and that we need his help to be an overcomer. We need to walk in God's grace and learn to walk by faith only. Now here are some scriptures to back up my points. You will notice that we are called by him only, not of our own seeking. He is knocking at everybody's hearts; your choice is to let him in.

My dear friend, this is what we follow if we are not saved or are walking in the flesh—human desires.

> Stand firm therefore in the liberty by which Christ has made us free, and don't be entangled again with a yoke of bondage. Behold, I, Paul, tell you that if you receive circumcision, Christ will profit you nothing. Yes, I testify again to every man who receives circumcision that he is a debtor to do the whole law. You are alienated

from Christ, you who desire to be justified by the law. You have fallen away from grace. For we, through the Spirit, by faith wait for the hope of righteousness. For in Christ Jesus neither circumcision amounts to anything, nor uncircumcision, but faith working through love. You were running well! Who interfered with you that you should not obey the truth? This persuasion is not from him who calls you. A little yeast grows through the whole lump. I have confidence toward you in the Lord that you will think no other way. But he who troubles you will bear his judgment, whoever he is. But I, brothers, if I still preach circumcision, why am I still persecuted? Then the stumbling block of the cross has been removed. I wish that those who disturb you would cut themselves off. For you, brothers, were called for freedom. Only don't use your freedom for gain to the flesh, but through love be servants to one another. For the whole law is fulfilled in one word, in this: "You shall love your neighbor as yourself." But if you bite and devour one another, be careful that you don't consume one another. But I say, walk by the Spirit, and you won't fulfill the lust of the flesh. For the flesh lusts against the Spirit, and the Spirit against the flesh; and these are contrary to one another, that you may not do the things that you desire. But if you are led by the Spirit, you are not under the law. Now the deeds of the flesh are obvious, which are: adultery, sexual immorality, uncleanness, lustfulness, idolatry, sorcery, hatred, strife, jealousies, outbursts of anger, rivalries, divisions, heresies, envy, murders, drunkenness, orgies, and things like these; of which I forewarn you, even as I also forewarned you, that those who practice such things will not inherit God's Kingdom. But the fruit of the Spirit is love, joy, peace, patience, kindness, goodness, faith, gentleness, and self-control. Against such things there is no law. Those who belong to Christ have crucified the flesh with its passions and lusts. If we live by the Spirit, let's also walk by the Spirit. Let's not become conceited, provoking one another, and envying one another. (Galatians 5 WEB)

I could write all day about what Jesus provided for us, but this is my life story. I want all people to know that even after God's Spirit comes into our lives, we will make mistakes in our choices in life and sometimes say or do the wrong things because of the spiritual states we allow in our life. Yes, we all make some bad choices, but God's grace and love will help us through it all. Read chapter 11 of Hebrews. All true followers walk by faith and in God's grace. Even though they did mighty work or saw mighty miracles in their life, everyone in God's Word also failed at times in their life. Look at King David. He was a man after God's own heart, yet he committed adultery and the murder of an innocent man.

CHAPTER 27

Part 2
Back in Wisconsin

The first thing I did was move back in with my parents in Milwaukee, Wisconsin, in June 1982. I started going to Elim Tabernacle, an Apostolic church. This was where God had me growing in my faith and learning to walk by faith and in his Spirit.

There was one thing that God impressed on me, an issue that was going to be a stumbling block to my walk in Christ. Whenever I would praise and worship God in spirit and in truth, Jesus would speak to me clear as day in my mind. He would say, *My child, you need to stop trusting your emotional feelings and stop expecting me to touch you all the time like I did when you were a child in Christ.*

We all know this. Those who are parents, when our children were babies, they needed constant attention. We held them a lot and showed them a lot of physical affection because they were very fragile and were too young to take care of themselves. But after you teach them how to walk, how to feed, and how to tell the difference between wrong and right, between what is good or what is evil, after a while they need to stop acting like a child and walk like a mature young person in the Lord. In other words, one does not always have parents to pamper you with affection; the physical contact becomes very minimal. You know enough about God that you need to trust him, regardless of your emotional state.

Yes, Jesus was telling me that he had proved to me in so many ways that he was a constant presence in my life and always provided for me, so that now I had to trust him daily without the physical contact and know he would be with me no matter how I felt. Of course, at this point of the conversation, I would resist that truth and try to tell God that I did not want to lose that physical feeling I had from him. So, of course, just like real parents still enforce new standards of life to help you mature on your own, God did the same.

What happened in my earlier days in my walk with Christ was going to have a serious conclusion that I wish would have never happened, because I did not take God's wisdom seriously about walking by faith, not by my feelings. These things are Christian stumbling blocks. Even today, too many Christians trust their feelings, not the Word of God alone. This causes many Christians to either fall in their walk or backslide until they accept God's grace by faith alone and stop being an emotional roller-coaster Christian. You will see why some things happened to me that, at the time, did not make godly sense and turned out to be very carnal choices and had some serious consequences on my life.

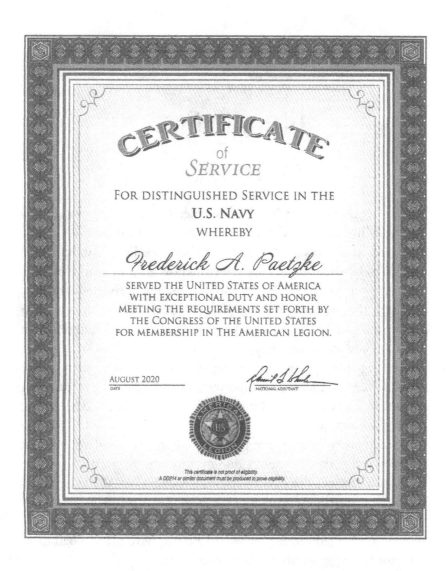

CHAPTER 28

Life with Carol

I was working at Big Boy at this time. This place was located by the Milwaukee airport on Layton Avenue. Carol was a waitress there, and I was a prep cook. I believe the Lord wanted me to lead her to Christ and help her grow in knowledge of him. However, because of our immature nature and my walking in the flesh at times, I thought that not only was she going to be a strong Christian, but God would give her to me for a wife. Yes, I should have prayed more about her and about that feeling I felt was from God. A lot of things were trying to stop me from going too far; even her parents were trying to keep us apart. Here God was, trying to stop me from doing something I was not ready for, but I thought it was the devil trying to keep us apart.

Since every one of our parents and friends tried to stop us, after being together for about one month, I took her to Madison, Wisconsin, to get her birth certificate, went to the downtown Milwaukee courthouse, and got married to her. I could not live in sin and have her living with me without her being my wife. Of course, if we had taken it slower, maybe we would not have made a bad decision, not knowing anything about each other.

One of the most glaring problems we had, besides the immaturity, was that we did not communicate with each other about each other. It was more like Carol never seemed to open up about her private life and desires and dreams. So in time, we drifted apart. I was more like a father figure to her than a husband, and she was just a follower of my choice, regardless of her feelings, which probably built up some resentment. It takes two for a marriage to work and last, or it will become dead. The lack of communication in our marriage was our downfall.

Let me say one thing more. What choice I made, I tried my best to make it last. I will always love her in Christ as one of my sisters in the faith. I believe Jesus still wants to take care of her and wants to take her to heaven someday. Also, I got two beautiful kids from that life we had together and grandkids from them, so all was not in vain. I am grateful that there are a lot of Bible characters who made some bad choices and that God still blessed the chosen to work out okay. Remember, all things work together for the good to them that love God and are called according to his purpose. With these opening statements, I will show how Jesus did a lot of miracles in our eleven years of marriage.

CHAPTER 29

God Make Himself Known

C arol and I were active in church. I was in prison ministry, and she helped in the church. Yes, Carol and I loved God. So God did some beautiful things in our lives. I taught a lot of Search for Truth Bible studies and had some home friendship gatherings. Jesus would do some special things when we gathered in his name. There was one time that we had a prayer request from Carol. She said to my brother Todd and me, "I have a boil that is causing me pain."

I said, "Carol, where is it?"

She showed us, and Todd and I prayed in the name of Jesus to heal her of that boil. Right before our eyes, the boil just vanished into nothing. It was as if it had been erased from her body, like it was never there. We all praised Jesus for healing her of that boil. At another Bible study again, God answered a prayer in two ways.

After Carol and I were married and living in South Milwaukee, Wisconsin, I worked for Patrick Cudahy. I paid all my bills at the time, and then I realized I did not have any money left for gas to get to work the rest of the week. So I called my brother in Christ to come over to talk. Todd came over, and we talked and prayed to God to be with us and help provide our needs according to his riches and glory.

See, at this time, I thought God would provide at least $5 from Todd. It would not be a miracle if I asked Todd for it, so I was waiting for God to tell him to help me. But before I knew it, my brother in Christ said he would be leaving soon. So I thought I'd help God out and said, "Todd, did Jesus tell you anything about me during our time together?"

He said, "Nothing out of the ordinary, things like lost loved ones and other spiritual needs."

Before I go any further, I will mention that I had looked for any money in my wallet, and it was empty; there was no cash at all. That's why I had invited my brother in Christ over. I could not take it any longer, and I said, "So, Todd, Jesus did not give you any desire to help me with a financial blessing?"

"No, Brother Rick. I am broke also."

I said, "You do not even have $5 to lend me?"

"No, brother. I am sorry that I cannot help you."

As Todd was talking to me, Jesus spoke to me in my heart, clear as day, and said, *You have $5 in your wallet, my son.*

I spoke to Jesus in my mind, saying, *Lord, you know I had no money in there before, but at your word, I will look again.* I said to Todd, "Do not worry about it. Jesus said he wants me to look in my wallet." I took it out, and I opened the cash part of the wallet. There it was, a brand-new $5 bill folded in thirds in my wallet, tucked in the corner of my billfold. I unfolded it, and everyone in the house praised God for providing me gas money for work. Then it hit me: when I was at church earlier that day, I had given the last of my money to God as an offering.

After Todd left, I went to the gas station and put the $5 in my gas tank for work. I had a Chevy car with an eight-cylinder engine, and I only had a quarter of a tank. So $5, I thought, would normally not be enough. I used over half a tank or more in a week's time. So I prayed, *Jesus, I need you to help my gas last until next Friday, on payday, so I can get more money to fill it up.* By the way, this was Sunday, so it had to take me to work for five days before I could cash my check and get more gas in the tank. By Wednesday, my gas tank was on "Empty" on the gauge, but I trusted the Lord for the rest of the week. Each day until Friday, I would nervously start the car, and it would get me to work and back.

Finally, Friday came, and empty as my tank looked, it still started and got me to work. After work, I took my check to cash it and then got to the nearest gas station. I was really freaked out, because as soon as I got to the pump, the car ran out of gas. I filled it up, and I was in great shape. God made it last on the $5 he provided for my faith in him to provide our needs. I praised God that day at the gas station.

CHAPTER 30

Miracles with My Car

There were a couple of times that I did errands with my car. One time, I was driving down Brown Deer Road, heading east. Carol, Sara (my eldest daughter), and I were in the car. We were on a three-lane road, heading east, coming up to a four-way intersection with turn signal lights on all four corners. As I was doing the speed limit of forty-five miles per hour, I got close to the four-way intersection. Our light was red, so my car and the others next to me on my right waited for the lights to turn green. In front of me, the left-turn lights turned on first, so cars going east and west could turn left before traffic on both sides could go straight through. The lights turned green for both sides to go forward on the street, and just before I started to move, Jesus spoke to my mind and said, *Do not go. The oncoming car going west will run the red light to turn south, and it will hit you.* So I did not move on green.

As the car on my left started to drive forward through the lit intersection, a car heading west and going south ran the turn signal that was solid red and ran into the other cars that had the right of way in front of me. Three cars were involved in the bad decision made by that driver. I would have had the worst impact of the car accidents, because my car would have hit him head-on if I had not listened to the voice of God. As I saw no major injuries, I drove around the cars that were involved and got to where I was heading.

Then there was a day where everything was going normally, and I was heading home from the north side of town and going to South Milwaukee. I was getting on the on-ramp on Good Hope Road. All of a sudden, my gas pedal went down, but the car engine could not get more gas to accelerate. The vehicle just would not move. As I coasted to my right to get out of the way of on-ramp traffic, I parked and put my flashers on and got out of my car to investigate the problem. I could not figure out how to get the gas pedal to work. I had no credit cards, no cash, and no phone to get help. I prayed, *Jesus, please help me get my family home so I can get my car to the shop for repairs.*

Within minutes, a car came out of nowhere and pulled up behind me. A man got out and walked over to me and said, "What is the problem?"

I said, "My gas pedal is not working right. I cannot accelerate the car."

He went under the hood, and in about ten minutes, he said, "Gas pedal spring was broken, so I temporarily got it to work until you get it fixed."

I said, "I am sorry, I cannot give you any money for your help."

He said, "Do not worry about it. The Lord takes care of his children."

I thought that was a strange thing to say to me, that the Lord watches his children. I never told him I was a believer, so it could be a coincidence. I got into my car and got ready to leave. The man who helped us was gone, but none of us saw him leave. However, it was true; my car started to work fine, and it kept on working until I got the money to fix the pedal.

I pulled into the repair shop on payday and parked it in the lot. The weird thing was, the mechanic went to pull the car into the garage and could not move it. He got out of the car and opened it and called me over to it. He said, "How did you get the car here?"

I said, "I drove it here."

"It should have been impossible. The gas pedal spring is completely broken and not long enough to reach the gas pedal."

"The man who helped us said he got the spring to work."

The repairman said, "I do not know what he used, but that spring, jury-rigged or not, would not be able to work."

I thanked God that day, knowing that the man on the highway was sent by him. Angel or man, he got me to where I needed to go until payday.

There was another time—or I should say, at least five times—that I got lost with my car or truck. Out of all these times, one time was an unexplained phenomenon to me that made no sense unless it was divine direction by God. I was going to a factory in Chicago, Illinois, a place I had never been to before. The directions I had written down could not be used because of road construction, so I had to get off the next exit five miles ahead.

Here I was, with no maps or a phone that had access to maps. I had a basic cheap phone from the nineties. I called the factory, and they were not taking any type of call. I had no money for maps, and no one had ever heard of that factory and street. So I prayed, *Jesus, please help me find this factory. Lord, you tell me when to turn, and I will trust you to get me there.*

The voice in my mind said, *Drive straight*, so I drove past a couple of blocks. The voice in my head said, *Go left. After a couple of blocks, turn right, and then after one block, turn left.*

At this point, I had no clue where I was. After about a mile, I turned right on this one street. After about two miles, the voice said, *Go right again*, so I turned right. As I went straight on that street for about two miles, there on my left was the factory where the pickup was. The good thing was, the on-ramp heading back to Milwaukee was two blocks away from the factory. So, yes, Jesus helped me find the business establishment and got me back home. God is a great GPS. Yes, if you have faith in God, he can help you when you are lost.

CHAPTER 31

Stopping a Suicide

I felt in my spirit that I had to move up to Ettrick, Wisconsin. First, I want to mention that we sometimes go to places Jesus really does not want us to go, and two things happen. One, you think God sent you somewhere, or two, you go against what the Holy Spirit directed anyway. Check out these two real Bible characters. One is Abraham, who went to a place like Egypt thinking that God would not mind; God had to bail him out of the troubles that came from not being where God really wanted him to be. Second is Jonah, who was told to go somewhere to help preach to Nineveh; he disobeyed God and went somewhere else.

> Now Yahweh's word came to Jonah the son of Amittai, saying, "Arise, go to Nineveh, that great city, and preach against it, for their wickedness has come up before me." But Jonah rose up to flee to Tarshish from the presence of Yahweh. He went down to Joppa, and found a ship going to Tarshish; so he paid its fare, and went down into it, to go with them to Tarshish from the presence of Yahweh. But Yahweh sent out a great wind on the sea, and there was a mighty storm on the sea, so that the ship was likely to break up. Then the mariners were afraid, and every man cried to his

god. They threw the cargo that was in the ship into the sea to lighten the ship. But Jonah had gone down into the innermost parts of the ship, and he was laying down, and was fast asleep. So the ship master came to him, and said to him, "What do you mean, sleeper? Arise, call on your God! Maybe your God will notice us, so that we won't perish." They all said to each other, "Come! Let's cast lots, that we may know who is responsible for this evil that is on us." So, they cast lots, and the lot fell on Jonah. Then they asked him, "tell us, please, for whose cause this evil is on us. What is your occupation? Where do you come from? What is your country? Of what people are you?" He said to them, "I am a Hebrew, and I fear Yahweh, the God of heaven, who has made the sea and the dry land." Then the men were exceedingly afraid, and said to him, "What have you done?" For the men knew that he was fleeing from the presence of Yahweh, because he had told them. Then they said to him, "What shall we do to you, that the sea may be calm to us?" For the sea grew more and more stormy. He said to them, "Take me up, and throw me into the sea. Then the sea will be calm for you; for I know that because of me this great storm is on you." Nevertheless the men rowed hard to get them back to the land; but they could not, for the sea grew more and more stormy against them. Therefore they cried to Yahweh, and said, "We beg you, Yahweh, we beg you, don't let us die for this man's life, and don't lay on us innocent blood; for you, Yahweh, have done as it pleased you." So they took up Jonah, and threw him into the sea; and the sea ceased its raging. Then the men feared Yahweh exceedingly; and they offered a sacrifice to Yahweh and made vows. Yahweh prepared a huge fish to swallow up Jonah, and Jonah was in the belly of the fish three days and three nights. (Jonah 1 WEB)

After Jonah repented, God had the big whale spit him out close to dry land right by Nineveh.

Let me start by saying that even if you go somewhere God did or did not send you, he will work around your choices to bring to pass his right will according to his purpose, not ours, for our own good. Of course, you may have some serious consequences like Jonah. The law of the harvest always comes to pass; what a man sows, he will also reap.

There was a time that I had a problem with a church up in Holmen, Wisconsin. I was going to a place I knew God would not like me to go normally, but at this time, he needed me to be at this place for a reason. It worked out for God's glory.

First things first, I believe true Christians should not drink or do any drugs. It opens the door for Satan to tempt you to do things not of God. I told Carol, my wife at the time, "I am going to the local tavern to chill out." You could say that I thought I was going where God would not want, but this time, God had other plans for me. I walked into the bar and sat down on a barstool close to a woman I had never met before. I called the bartender over to me and said, "Could I have a tap beer, please?" He said sure and gave me the choice I asked for.

Believe it or not, even when I am running from God or trying to avoid talking to him, I would whisper things to God under my breath. As I saw my beer, I said to God, "Jesus, I am sorry, but I am really upset about how this thing turned out at church. I think the issue I had was handled unfairly." For a minute or so, I complained to Jesus about my problems under my breath. After a couple of minutes, maybe seven or so, I had nothing going through my mind; I was pretty much staring out into space, looking straight ahead of me. Then a strange thing happened.

Jesus said, *Talk to that woman next to you.*

I said, "I am married, and I do not feel like talking to her." I was not sure if the devil was setting me up or if my thoughts were going crazy.

Again, a voice in my head said, *Talk to her.*

I asked why.

Jesus said, *Tell her not to commit suicide and that I really love her.*

My mind was racing. I was thinking, *Am I going crazy? What will happen if it's not Jesus talking to me? She will think I am a crazy person.*

So I tried to ignore the voice of God in my soul, but God spoke loudly in my mind, *Talk to her now.*

I finally gave in and spoke to her. I said to her, "Hi, my name is Rick. I am a Christian chaplain, and I believe in God. First, faithful Christians do not go to bars. I am what the church calls a backslider currently. But I feel that God wants me to say this to you. First of all, Jesus still loves you, and two, he said please do not commit suicide. He has plans for you."

I was thinking, *I hope this is not me imagining things not of God,* but after I said that to her, she slowly looked up at me and stared right at me. "What did you say?"

I repeated what God said about him loving her and telling her not to kill herself.

After I said it the second time, she started to cry out loud. I was thinking, *I did it. Now she is going to say I am crazy.* But no, she said, "Yes, I told God before I got to this bar that if he does not tell me that he loves me, I will commit suicide today. Then you come in and tell me something about myself that no one knew. I am thankful that you listened to God. What should I do now?"

I said, "Let us get out of here and pray right now."

She agreed. I took her to my car, and we prayed her through to Jesus and got her sins forgiven. She fully gave her life to Christ. God filled her with his Holy Spirit, and she was totally happy. I told her about some churches to go to, and I told her to get a Bible and read it and pray every day, for God had great plans for her life. I dropped her off and went home and told my wife about how God used me in a place I never dreamed God would use me.

It has happened at least three times; there were two other bars where I witnessed about Jesus dying for other people's sins. Yes, Jesus went to the publicans and sinners to give them the good news of salvation.

CHAPTER 32

Daughter Almost Drowns

One day, in the summer, I felt like going fishing, so I asked my wife if she wanted to go. She said, "No, but I would like to visit Mary, Bob's wife."

"Sounds great."

So Carol and my daughter followed me out to the car, and we drove out to my cousin Bob's house.

I asked if Bob wanted to go fishing on the Wisconsin Trempealeau lock and dam on the Mississippi River. Arthur, the oldest boy of Mary, asked if they could go swimming in the river close to where we were going to fish. Bob and I said, "Sure. You, Louie, the other two boys, and Sara (my daughter) could go with us." So we packed up the kids and went fishing.

There was one thing I was not thinking about. The river had a lot of drop-offs and strong currents close to where the kids would go swimming, so one of the adults should have kept an eye on them. But, no, Bob and I were too young in our thinking and more concerned about fishing that we let a young boy named Arthur, who was only twelve at the time, watch all four kids as they swam. Those kids were little Robert Jr., Louie, Matt, and my daughter, Sara. Jesus only knows if Arthur knew how to swim. I want to thank Jesus first for even watching over my daughter, who was only nine at the time, and my young nephews, who were swimming in this dangerous river. Yes, there was a beach area, but the river was marked where the dangerous

141

parts were; we forgot to tell the kids where not to go swimming and what not to get close to.

So Bob and I went to the lock and dam to fish, told the kids where we were going, and said, "Let us know when you guys are done with swimming." Yes, I should have kept an eye on my kid, but the grace of God watched over them. I am glad that I pray for my kids every day, because you never know what they will face in life day by day. I remember how accident-prone I was as a child. What was I thinking?

What happened was, while the young boys were swimming close to the shore, my daughter, Sara, decided to wander off to the buoys, which marked the drop-offs to the deep water and strong currents. As my little girl got close to the buoys, she walked to a part of the river that dropped off deep. She started to drown and panic, trying to get back to solid ground, and she thought, *God, please help me. Otherwise, I will be with you soon.* At that moment, God spoke to Arthur's mind and said, *Quick, grab Sara, your cousin. She cannot swim where she's at.* Arthur got close to her as fast as he could and grabbed her shirt over her swim trunks and pulled her to a safe depth where she could stand on her own. I venture that after this, she never tried to go to the dangerous parts again.

Of course, the kids still swam and played there until we stopped fishing and went home. I never noticed that the T-shirt Sara wore was missing all that time. They tried to tell us that Sara almost drowned, and we just blew it off, thinking that kids make up some crazy stories for attention. It is sad that I never knew this truth about God sparing my daughter's life, until I started to write my life story, and I am in my fifties now. Yes, praise Jesus that, like he saved me from drowning, he did the same for my little girl.

CHAPTER 33

My Son Is Born

I will say one thing before I get into the story. There are two points behind why marriages fail and couples break it off with each other. One is that the two people have a communication problem in their relationship. This is when one or both parties stop talking to each other about their feelings and other things, which hurts both companions. The second problem we all must deal with is our own sinful nature that we all are born with. Yes, even after our new birth, we must still deal with the fleshly things we grew up with. The main way our bodies are wired is, we are very self-centered beings, and if not kept in check by God, we do things only to please ourselves first, not caring who we hurt to get it. Yes, we all fall into this trap at times; therefore, we need to be led by the Holy Spirit daily.

You can understand why my first wife and I did not work out. Also, we got married too young and knew each other not long enough. Yes, one month is not enough time to really know someone. I was married that fast. We stopped talking to each other after about a year's time. At that time, we tried not to think about each other, but we never got a divorce. Yes, God tried to get us back together. I moved back to Milwaukee and tried to live for God the best I could.

One day, my wife, Carol, came over, and we talked about getting back with each other for our daughter's sake and for the better of our Christian walk. So we got an apartment in the city and tried to work on our marriage. After a few months, my wife said, "I need to tell you something, but I am afraid you will get mad."

"What's up? You can tell me. God will help me," I said, not knowing what I was about to hear.

"I am pregnant again."

I said, "That's all? That's good news. God is giving us a new start with a baby. That's a good thing. Why would you think that would make me mad?"

Carol said, "That's not my problem. It's that I'm not sure if the baby is yours or not."

I said, "That's crazy. You are newly pregnant. The time we've been together only means it's our child, because you and I are the only ones having relations. Is there something you are not telling me?"

"Yes. I am sorry, but I still had a relationship with that older man."

I said, "How is that?"

"When you went to work, he would come over at times."

That was like a knife in my heart; I was stunned. I said, "Let us try to get past this then. What did your other friend say when you told him you're pregnant?"

"He broke it off and split."

Well, I tried my best to move on with our life, but the nine months came quick. She was about to deliver the child, and she said, "Rick, I need to go to the hospital. It's time."

As we drove to the hospital, the devil tormented my mind and said to my heart, *How can you love that baby? It might not even be your child. How would you feel if you see Carol's old flame in him or her?* Those thoughts of her betrayal flooded my mind, so I said, "I am too messed up to watch the birth, because if this child looks like the other man's baby, I do not know how I will react." I dropped her off at the hospital and said, "Call me when you're done."

I got back to the apartment and sat in my recliner, and I did not realize that I fell into a deep sleep or a dream. I'm not sure. I thought I was awake. Before I knew it, I was walking into Carol's hospital room, and she was pushing the child out. Her mother was there also, and the doctor and a nurse were in the room. I was thinking to myself, *Why am I here? I said I would not be coming here, but here I am.* Then the doctor told Carol to push, and her mother was encouraging her to push. Before I knew it, the doctor said, "I see the baby crowning. Give it another push." Then out came the baby. The doctor said, "Mr. Paetzke, would you like to hold your newborn son?" I thought, *What will happen if it looks like someone else's kid?* Then the doctor said, "The baby looks like his father," and he handed me my son. As I looked at the boy, he looked just like I did when I was a child. At this time, I heard bells ringing in the background. I was thinking, *Whose phone is ringing?*

Then all of a sudden, I woke up from my sleep. My apartment phone was ringing, so I picked it up. It was Carol on the phone. She said, "Can you come to the hospital?" At that point, God spoke to my mind and said, *Go see your son.* So I shot up, got my car keys, and headed to St. Mary's Hospital. I prayed, *Jesus, help me accept whatever I see. I'm still not sure what the baby will look like.* I asked God to help me love the child regardless of what would happen. So God did just that.

First, everything I heard in my dream was coming out of everybody's mouth—what Carol said, what the doctor said, and what Carol's mother said. It was very surreal. I was like, *How did I hear everybody say these exact words before?* But one part God put into the story that was not in the dream was my caring, loving heart for this child.

Just before the baby was born, the doctor cried out that the umbilical cord was wrapped around the baby's head, and he said, "If I do not get this cord off his neck, this baby will die." So I ran to the chapel and cried out to the Lord and said, "Jesus, please spare my baby. I promise I will love him no matter what."

After about five minutes, God spoke to my mind and said, *He will be all right.*

So I went to the room where Carol was, and just as I walked into the room, the baby flipped itself out of the cord wrapped around its neck. It was a miracle. God caused the child to flip over, and the cord came off the child's neck. Remember, in the dream I had, the point where the baby flipped in my wife's womb was where the dream started and was the point just before I got to the hospital.

"Push, Carol! The baby is almost out!" With a quick push from Carol, out came my son. The doctor said, "Mr. Paetzke, would you like to hold your son?"

I said, "Sure, okay."

I looked at the baby boy wrapped in a blanket, and he looked just like me in my dream, with the exact proportions and details. Of course, tears ran down my cheeks as God said not to worry. *He is your real son, not the other man's baby.* The older he grew, the more I saw myself in that boy. I never needed a blood test to prove it.

CHAPTER 34

Many Jobs

Yes, my friends, I had different types of jobs. I was never picky early in my life; I believed that whatever job I found, I would accept it for my livelihood. Yes, God said that if a man does not work, he should not eat. I'm paraphrasing the Word. Yes, I worked in restaurants, factories, and parcel services, mostly working with people because I wanted to help people know Jesus Christ, if possible.

There were two jobs I had that, without a doubt, I knew Jesus helped me get. One was Patrick Cudahy, a meatpacking house. I prayed to God and said, "Lord, where should I apply today?" Within minutes, Patrick Cudahy came to my mind. I called the meatpacking house and asked if they were taking applications at all. They were, so I went to the human resources department and filled out an application. Trusting that Jesus was going to get me the job, I asked the secretary if I could talk to the person who did the hiring. She said, "He might be busy. I will get this application to him, and we will call you if something opens."

I said, "Please go and get him. I really need this job."

She sighed and went to the human resources manager and asked him. He relented and asked me to his office. He introduced himself, and I did the same. He said, "Please take a seat." He looked over my application and asked me if I had any experience working at a meat-packing house.

"No, not much, but I am a fast learner. I will do anything you give me to do."

"Well," he said, "we are not hiring for any position at this time, so I will keep your paperwork on file."

Without thinking, I blurted out, "I know you will hire me, because Jesus said you will give me a job."

He said, "I admire your faith, but nothing is available at this time."

I said, "It's okay. A job will open for me tomorrow." I said goodbye and that we would talk tomorrow.

He replied, "We will see."

The next day came, and before noon, I felt led to call the factory. I asked if I could talk to the manager again. He came to the phone and said, "This is the manager. How can I help you?"

I said, "This is Frederick Paetzke. When do I start my new job?"

He was stunned and said he would call me if something opened up.

I said, "Okay, I will talk to you later today," and said goodbye.

Before 3:00 p.m., my phone rang. My mother told me it was the packing house on the phone. I ran to the phone and said, "Hello, this is Mr. Paetzke."

He said, "Mr. Paetzke, a job just opened for general labor. Come in tomorrow at 8:00 a.m. You will make $6.50 per hour."

That was good for pay at the time. Now I could get a place for me and my family to live.

Years later, I needed a job again, and I applied at Raabe, the paints company. I started October 21, 1993. Wherever I worked, I tried my best to be a Christian example to all my coworkers. So whenever I was on break or off-duty, if Jesus put it in my heart to talk about him to my coworkers, I would tell them about Jesus dying for their sins and any other things God put in my heart to share. One thing I found out was that when you do this, you get the devil mad, and you start getting persecuted for your faith.

I was learning the job particularly well, and I was a hard worker. I never called in sick and never complained. You needed to work past ninety days to keep your job, and on December 20, 1993, one day before my probation period ended, I was called in to my supervisor's office after work. He asked me to have a seat, and he said, "You're a great worker, and it's been an honor to have you with this company. But we need a team player to work together here."

I said, "I have no complaints about my coworkers."

He said, "I know you work well with all, but two women workers do not want to work with you. They said if you stay, they will quit. And we cannot afford to lose two employees for one. I am sorry, I will have to let you go."

I was incredibly sad and said, "How am I supposed to give my kids a good Christmas without a job to bring in income?"

He said, "I am sorry. I wish you the best, and if you need a good work reference, let me know."

When I got home, I told my wife that I lost my job, and I said, "Until I find a job, we will not be able to get the kids Christmas presents this year, because we need to pay rent. Only God can provide gifts for the kids." So I prayed, "Jesus, please help me figure out how to get my kids something for Christmas."

The next day, I got a phone call from Raabe's union representative, and he asked me, "Why did they let you go one day before your probationary period was over?"

I explained that I felt it was because of my faith. "They would not tell me why, but they said two women did not like working with me. So they let me go instead."

He said that if he had known they were trying that, he could have helped me get my job back. However, the company had me sign a job waiver, so his hands were tied.

I said, "It's okay. God will provide. I pray that God will help me give my kids a nice Christmas day. The Lord's will be done."

The next day came. It was Christmas Eve, and I was walking around my home and talking to the Lord in prayer. Something made me have the desire to look out to the street from our upper window. I saw a man and a woman come out of their car, and they had three big garbage bags of stuff in their hands. They walked up to my house and rang the doorbell.

My wife said, "Who's at the door?"

I said, "I am not sure. A couple came to the door, but I do not know them. I will go down and check it out."

I went downstairs and opened the door. I said, "How can I help you folks?"

They said, "Are you Fred Paetzke?"

"Yes."

"I am the man who talked to you on the phone."

I said, "Nice to meet you and your wife. What brings you to my home?"

They said, "The Lord put it in our heart to give your family good Christmas supplies."

I said, "Praise God and all who donated for my family! I now can show how God provides for us when we let our light shine in a dark world."

Yes, the Lord blessed my whole family with a lot of food and clothes and even enough gifts for my son and daughter. Yes, God provided for us a good Christmas day.

CHAPTER 35

Dark Days Ahead

Months later, I felt God was leading me to move from Milwaukee. God was already blessing my prison ministry, and I felt close to him at this time. The adversary sent me a big temptation about starting a church somewhere without seeking God's will and getting some godly counsel, and after this, my life and marriage fell apart. Keep this in mind: throughout the Bible, there are true stories of people of faith at times getting out of God's will for their lives. Some did not seek God out about their final choice, which cost them something in their lives. The Word says that all things work together for good to them that love God and are called according to his purpose, for where sin did abound, God's grace did much more abound. We all have free will in our lives, but when we choose wrong, we reap what we sow in life.

I thank God that Jesus still helps you your whole lifetime here on earth. If you're living here in this present life, it's plain that Jesus is trying to reach out to the lost world through the children of God. Jesus paid for all our sins in our lifetime; we must accept his offering for our lives to avoid judgment. We must let Jesus control our life every day of our lives to overcome the evil in this world.

So that I can move on with my story, there were things that changed my life. One, God was not the one who led me to move. Why do I know this? Because when I moved, I lost my job, the church never got started, and nothing but chaos happened. I told my wife, "We need to move back to Milwaukee, Wisconsin." She would not go. I said, "I will go and send for you when I get a job if God is calling me back to Milwaukee." But a couple of weeks later, after I found a good job and a place to move to, my wife divorced me, and I lost my kids. However, in time, God gave me my daughter to live with me when it was all final.

Years after my first wife left me, Jesus still showed me his grace and helped me heal after all my bad choices. In time, God let me remarry. I married my present wife, who really loves God and is my best helpmate in this world. These are my stories on our life together.

CHAPTER 36

Fresh Start

I prayed for a good wife, and in time, Jesus let Christine come into my life. At the time, she was not a sold-out Christian yet, but in time, God would open her eyes; she would fall in love with God and his Word.

I remember that at the time I first met her and took her home, I never mentioned anything to her about God in my life. But she said something to me that blew me away. First, she said that she had been diagnosed with crippling arthritis. She was unable to move until God healed her so she could walk, and he put it in remission. I thought, *If she only knew what I have seen regarding God in my life.* She even knew that we were going to be a married couple someday. Deep thought on this statement. She did say to me, "Rick, will you marry me?" Most men on their first date at this point would run away on this statement, but I ponder those thoughts in my heart.

To my fellow readers, it is important to realize that we all fail in life. There are not any perfect people or born-again believers who do not sin or fail at times. I was what a Christian calls a backslider. A prodigal son is what I call it. In the story of the two sons living with their father, both knew what their father expected his sons to follow in life. However, one of them got frustrated and went to a distant city far from home, to live his life the way he pleased. He thought his dad's rules were way too strict for him. But deep inside himself, he knew his father's ways were correct. That's why he moved far away from his family. Even though the son left was in the wrong, his brother at home was not much better in his actions. The son at home was a self-righteous person who only care about himself. He was backslidden and did not even know it. The one at home was very religious, very judgmental, and legalistic, just like the Pharisees of the day were. Here are some scriptures to prove my point.

What then? Are we better than they? No, in no way. For we previously warned both Jews and Greeks that they are all under sin. As it is written "There is no one righteous no, not one. There is no one who understands. There is no one who seeks after God. They have all turned away. They have together become unprofitable. There is no one who does good, no, not so much as one. (Romans 3:9–12 WEB)

Therefore you are without excuse, O man, whoever you are who judge. For in that which you judge another, you condemn yourself. For you who judge practice the same things. We know that the judgment of God is according to truth against those who practice such things. Do you think this, O man who judges those who practice such things, and do the same, that you will escape the judgment of God? Or do you despise the riches of his goodness, forbearance, and patience, not knowing that the goodness of God leads you to repentance? (Romans 2:1–4)

Yes, we all need God's Spirit to help us live day by day. We must die to the self and let Christ live in us every day. Not my will but your will be done, Father, in heaven and earth. Now read the prodigal son story and notice that both sons have some bad thinking going on in their lives.

He said, "A certain man had two sons. The younger of them said to his father, 'Father, give me my share of your property.' So he divided his livelihood between them. Not many days after, the younger son gathered all of this together and traveled into a far country. There he wasted his property with riotous living. When he had spent all of it, there arose a severe famine in that country, and he began to be in need. He went and joined himself to one of the citizens of that country, and he sent him into his fields to feed pigs. He wanted to fill his belly with the husks that the pigs ate, but no one gave him any. But when he came to himself, he said, 'How many hired servants of my father's have bread enough to spare, and I'm dying with hunger! I will get up and go to my father, and will tell him, "Father, I have sinned against heaven, and in your sight. I am no more worthy to be called your son. Make me as one of your hired servants."'

"He arose and came to his father. But while he was still far off, his father saw him, and was moved with compassion, and ran, and fell on his neck, and kissed him. The son said to him, 'Father, I have sinned against heaven and in your sight. I am no longer worthy to be called your son.' "But the father said to his servants, 'Bring out the best robe, and put it on him. Put a ring on his hand, and sandals on his feet. Bring the fattened calf, kill it, and let's eat, and celebrate; for this, my son, was dead, and is alive again. He was lost and is found.' Then they began to celebrate.

"Now his elder son was in the field. As he came near to the house, he heard music and dancing. He called one of the servants to him and asked what was going on. He said to him, 'Your brother has come, and your father has killed the fattened calf, because he has received him back safe and healthy.' But he was angry, and would not go in. Therefore, his father came out, and begged him. But he answered his father, 'Behold, these many years I have served you, and I never disobeyed a commandment of yours, but you never gave me a goat, that I might celebrate with my friends. But when this your son came, who has devoured your living with prostitutes, you killed the fattened calf for him.'

"He said to him, 'Son, you are always with me, and all that is mine is yours. But it was appropriate to celebrate and be glad, for this, your brother, was dead, and is alive again. He was lost and is found. (Luke 15:11–32)

CHAPTER 37

❦

Divorce

I felt that I was not welcome back in my old church.

At first, the church family was happy to see me, but when they found out I was a divorced man, they did not know how to relate to me, knowing that my first wife had left me. They would not go out of their way to accept me, so they avoided me altogether. Because I was being isolated, I felt I was a total failure as a Christian. I thought I was a hypocrite and thought I had committed an unpardonable sin, and I stopped going to church. I let Satan deceive me into believing a total lie, and I ran from my God, who never stopped loving me.

I thank God that where sin did abound, God's grace did much more abound. Yes, Jesus died for all my sins, past, present, and future ones. Of course, we are not to keep sinning just to get more grace; we need to die to our old ways day by day. Until we die, our old nature will wrestle with our new nature until we are in a glorified body. Yes, when you fall away or give up on your Christian journey, it is gradual; it does not happen overnight.

So in time, I stopped reading the Bible, stopped praying, and tuned out God's Holy Spirit. Then I found myself drinking again, smoking cigarettes, and doing different types of drugs, such as pills, crack cocaine, pot—basically doing everything in life to please myself only. The saddest thing is, if you're like me, as a backslider you realize that you are the most depressed person on earth. No one can run from Jesus and be happy, so you try to drown out the Spirit calling you home, using anything to drown out his voice. You find out also that the people around you who are not God's children couldn't care less if you live or die. But there are people who are of God who care and love you and want God's best for you.

To all who read this, saved or unsaved, Jesus will always love you regardless of how many mistakes you make. That is why he died for us. He knows how imperfect we are; that's why we need to submit our will to his will in our lives, so day by day, he can renew us in his image and likeness. It is like a lump of clay in a potter's hands. The clay is a big patch of ugly dirt and water, but the potter turns the mass into a beautiful masterpiece. After he gets it off the potter's wheel, he paints it and puts on certain decorations, and he shows it off to the people around him. We, like clay, have a lot of impurities and garbage in our bodies that God needs to work out of us daily until he is finished with us. That will be at our death.

One of the tools that the potter uses is fire to burn off the bad parts of the clay. He also uses sharp knives to cut things out of the clay, and much more work goes into the clay before it's ready to be the final product we all see. To become a child of God, we need to become a new lump of clay so Jesus can make us a new creation.

There were seven to eight years of bad things I allowed back into my life that Jesus had to purge out of my life again, but he did it. If I let him make me a new vessel for his glory, everything will work itself out for my good. So when I gave myself back to God and asked him to set me free from all bad sins and habits, like drugs, alcohol, and cigarettes, he set me free. I have been free for over fifteen years now. One habit was hard to break, but later, I will tell you about how he broke the addiction in my life. Here is proof of what Jesus does with all his children.

> The word which came to Jeremiah from Jehovah, saying, Arise, and go down to the potter's house, and there I will cause thee to hear my words. Then I went down to the potter's house, and behold, he was making a work on the wheels. And when the vessel that he made of the clay was marred in the hand of the potter, he made it

again another vessel, as seemed good to the potter to make it. Then the word of Jehovah came to me, saying, O house of Israel, cannot I do with you as this potter? saith Jehovah. Behold, as the clay in the potter's hand, so are ye in my hand, O house of Israel. At what instant I shall speak concerning a nation, and concerning a kingdom, to pluck up and to break down and to destroy it; if that nation, concerning which I have spoken, turn from their evil, I will repent of the evil that I thought to do unto them. And at what instant I shall speak concerning a nation, and concerning a kingdom, to build and to plant it; if they do that which is evil in my sight, that they obey not my voice, then I will repent of the good, wherewith I said I would benefit them. Now therefore, speak to the men of Judah, and to the inhabitants of Jerusalem, saying, Thus saith Jehovah: Behold, I frame evil against you, and devise a device against you: return ye now everyone from his evil way, and amend your ways and your doings. But they say, it is in vain; for we will walk after our own devices, and we will do every one after the stubbornness of his evil heart. (Jeremiah 18:1–12 ASV)

"Your hands have framed me and fashioned me altogether, yet you destroy me. Remember, I beg you, that you have fashioned me as clay. Will you bring me into dust again? (Job 10:8–9 WEB)

If you refuse to become a child of God and are not born of above, you will not go to heaven. You must submit to the Potter's hands to be saved.

But indeed, O man, who are you to reply against God? Will the thing formed ask him who formed it, "Why did you make me like this?" Or hasn't the potter a right over the clay, from the same lump to make one part a vessel for honor, and another for dishonor? What if God, willing to show his wrath and to make his power known, endured with much patience vessels of wrath prepared for destruction, and that he might make known the riches of his glory on vessels of mercy, which he prepared beforehand for glory, us, whom he also called, not from the Jews only, but also from the Gentiles? (Romans 9:20–24)

Count it all joy, my brothers, when you fall into various temptations, knowing that the testing of your faith produces endurance. Let endurance have its perfect work, that you may be perfect and complete, lacking in nothing. (James 1:2–4)

Therefore, since Christ suffered for us in the flesh, arm yourselves also with the same mind; for he who has suffered in the flesh has ceased from sin, that you no longer should live the rest of your time in the flesh for the lusts of men, but for the will of God. For we have spent enough of our past time doing the desire of the Gentiles, and having walked in lewdness, lusts, drunken binges, orgies, carousings, and abominable idolatries. They think it is strange that you don't run with them into the same excess of riot, blaspheming. They will give account to him who is ready to judge the living and the dead. For to this end the Good News was preached even to the dead, that they might be judged indeed as men in the flesh, but live as to God in the spirit. But the end of all things is near. Therefore be of sound mind, self-controlled, and sober in prayer. And above all things be earnest in your love among yourselves, for love covers a multitude of sins. Be hospitable to one another without grumbling. As each has received a gift, employ it in serving one another, as good managers of the grace of God in its various forms. If anyone speaks, let it be as it were the very words of God. If anyone serves, let it be as of the strength which God supplies, that in all things God may be glorified through Jesus Christ, to whom belong the glory and the dominion forever and ever. Amen. Beloved don't be astonished at the fiery trial which has come upon you to test you, as though a strange thing happened to you. But because you are partakers of Christ's sufferings, rejoice, that at the revelation of his glory you also may rejoice with exceeding joy. If you are insulted for the name of Christ, you are blessed; because the Spirit of glory and of God rests on you. On their part he is blasphemed, but on your part, he is glorified. For let none of you suffer as a murderer, or a thief, or an evil doer, or a meddler in other men's matters. But if one of you suffers for being a Christian, let him not be ashamed; but let him glorify God in this matter. For the time has come for judgment to begin with the household of God. If it begins first with us, what will happen to those who don't obey the Good News of God? "If it is hard for the righteous to be saved, what will happen to the ungodly and the sinner?" Therefore let them also who suffer according to the will of God in doing good entrust their souls to him, as to a faithful Creator. (1 Peter 4)

If good people barely make it, what is in store for the bad?

So if you find life difficult because you are doing what God said, take it in stride. Trust him. He knows what he is doing, and he will keep on doing it. Let Jesus put you on his potter's wheel, and live with him forever here and in the afterlife. When you pray to your heavenly Father, ask him in Jesus's name to forgive you for all your sins, and state to him that you believe that he rose again on the third day for your sin's total forgiveness. Ask and believe in him that he will come into your being and fill you with the baptism of the Holy Spirit, and start to praise him for saving your soul and delivering you from death to life everlasting. Then read your Bible daily and pray to God every day and find a Holy Spirit–led church to grow in Christ.

> Behold, I stand at the door and knock. If anyone hears my voice and opens the door, then I will come in to him, and will dine with him, and he with me. He who overcomes, I will give to him to sit down with me on my throne, as I also overcame, and sat down with my Father on his throne. (Revelation 3:20–21)

CHAPTER 38

———◇———

Drowning in Pewaukee Lake

I n July 2000, on a nice sunny morning, Christine, my son Kevin, and I went fishing around 6:00 a.m. After a couple of hours, my son wanted to go swimming, so I dropped him off at the beach. Just Christine and I went out to fish more on the lake. My son was ten years old, and I let him go swimming since the beach had a lifeguard on duty. Of course, this helped me know he was safe from what was going to happen soon after.

I was fishing on this nice sunny day. It was a little breezy but not too bad, though the deeper side of the lake had a very steady wind blowing. The lake was exceptionally large, so sailboats could use it also. On certain days, they would have sailboat races, and I had no clue that they had one going on that Saturday afternoon. After about an hour passed of me fishing for panfish or bass close to the big island on the lake, there was not much action from both fish species, so I thought, *Hey, I will try fishing somewhere on the deeper side of the lake.*

My dear reader, keep this in mind: my girlfriend at the time was sitting on a boat cushion, but she had the life jacket next to her, as it was hard to fish with it on. Christine, at this time, had a bad case of crippling arthritis. This meant she could not swim. Of course, I treated her as if she could swim. I did not bother asking her if she was able to swim, because we were not expecting to flip the boat over.

So I told Christine, "Let's go over to the deeper side of the lake to see if we can catch any fish there." I started the boat's motor and headed for the deep side of the lake. As we drew closer to the deep side, a motorboat came close to us and said, "Fishing on this side of the lake is off-limits while sailboats are racing."

I answered, "Okay, I did not know that."

As the motorboat took off, I talked to Christine, saying, "We need to turn around and find a place on the lower part of the lake again."

But before I could turn the boat around, I noticed two huge sailboats heading toward us. One passed us on the left side of the boat, and the other on the right side, just a couple of seconds apart. Just as the boats passed us, I noticed two huge waves coming at us from both sides of the boat. I cried out, "Chrissy, hang on! I think the boat might flip over!" Before I could steer the boat to safety, it completely flipped over. As the waves crashed on both sides, I cried out, "Jesus, help me be okay!" It happened so fast that, as the boat flipped over, I found myself not even going underwater but being safe and holding on to the bottom of the siding. I thanked Jesus for not allowing me to go underwater.

About ten seconds passed, and it hit me that my girlfriend was not coming up out of the water. She was underneath the boat, slowly sinking to the bottom of the lake. I could not tell where in the lake she was. I was very scared and worried that she was going to drown. Not knowing what to do, I prayed out loud, "Jesus, please do not let her drown. She still needs to be born again of your Spirit. She's not ready to die. I would not be able to live with myself if she drowns."

Just after I prayed that prayer, I noticed a pontoon boat heading our way. But before they reached us, I saw my girlfriend come up out of the water like a bullet, so fast that half her body left the water. As she came down to water level, I grabbed her hand and held on until the pontoon boat came and pulled her up first, then me. They towed us to Smokey's Bait Shop, where we dropped off the boat, and our fishing trip was over. We packed up what we had left from the boat into the car and picked up my son.

As we were heading home, I was still numb, thinking of how blessed we were that no one drowned. Christine was telling my son, "Your dad is a hero. He was so strong that he swam under the boat, down deep in the water, and grabbed me by the arm and placed his hand on top of my shoulder to keep it from dislocating from the joint (because of her fused joints)." It suddenly hit me as we were driving home that either Jesus or an angel had saved my girlfriend. I said to her in the car that it was not me or anyone else around who dove in to bring her up and keep her from sinking to the bottom of the lake. With a stunned look on all our faces, we realized that God had just performed a miracle in our lives. Praise God! In time, Christine became a true child of God because of that miracle. It made her realize how real God is in today's world.

CHAPTER 39

Was Lost, Now Found

C hurch, I urge you to follow the Shepherd and make the Word of God your nutrient-rich meal. Listen to his voice, eat his Word, and follow him. Reader, if you are not born again after the Holy Spirit, you are a goat. But I have great news. With the help of Jesus Christ, you can be born into a new sheep, a new creature in Christ. Follow the Good Shepherd today.

It was around January 1995. First, the most dangerous thing a Christian can do is walk with God based on his emotion-filled life. It is a faith walk, not a feeling walk. If you trust your feelings in your dark days, you will fall. Trust in God's Word in everything you do, or you will become a double-minded Christian.

> He is a double-minded man, unstable in all his ways. (James 1:8 WEB)

> I hate double-minded men, but I love your law. (Psalm 119:113)

> Count it all joy, my brothers, when you fall into various temptations, knowing that the testing of your faith produces endurance. Let endurance have its perfect work, that you may be perfect and complete, lacking in nothing. But if any

of you lacks wisdom, let him ask of God, who gives to all liberally and without reproach, and it will be given to him. But let him ask in faith, without any doubting, for he who doubts is like a wave of the sea, driven by the wind and tossed. For that man shouldn't think that he will receive anything from the Lord. He is a double-minded man, unstable in all his ways. But let the brother in humble circumstances glory in his high position; and the rich, in that he is made humble, because like the flower in the grass, he will pass away. For the sun arises with the scorching wind and withers the grass, and the flower in it falls, and the beauty of its appearance perishes. So the rich man will also fade away in his pursuits. Blessed is a person who endures temptation, for when he has been approved, he will receive the crown of life, which the Lord promised to those who love him. Let no man say when he is tempted, "I am tempted by God," for God can't be tempted by evil, and he himself tempts no one. But each one is tempted when he is drawn away by his own lust and enticed. Then the lust, when it has conceived, bears sin. The sin, when it is full grown, produces death. Don't be deceived, my beloved brothers. Every good gift and every perfect gift is from above, coming down from the Father of lights, with whom can be no variation, nor turning shadow. Of his own will he gave birth to us by the word of truth, that we should be a kind of first fruits of his creatures. (James 1:2–18)

Now you are aware of how to think as a child of God. I did what a Christian should never do. After my wife divorced me, I felt alienated from the church I was going to and was emotionally down about my wife leaving me for another person. I was a basket case of hurt and lonely feelings. I decided to look for a woman to help me not feel alone. Instead of trusting God for a good wife, I took the wrong path to find a wife in the world, not from the body of Christ. I thank God that even with the wrong path I chose, he led me to a woman named Christine, whom he wanted to save from the world.

At first, I tried to talk to her about my faith in Jesus Christ and how he helped me through life. But like Adam did in the Bible, I chose to follow the path my lady friend wanted to go. I thought, *Someday she will need God. Then I will tell her more.* But Jesus had other plans for us both. If you think that in this life you can make it without Jesus's help, you are in a losing battle. We were created to follow him to succeed. If not, you will always fall into a ditch. The bad thing is, our old sinful nature is clueless about God's path in life, so when we follow our carnal, selfish desires, it takes us down. Instead of being led by the Holy Spirit, I trusted the dead nature of man.

> For all that is in the world, the lust of the flesh, the lust of the eyes, and the pride of life, isn't the Father's, but is the world's. The world is passing away with its lusts, but he who does God's will remains forever. (1 John 2:16–17)

So in about nine years' time, I was totally a backslider, swearing and drinking hard liquor. In time, Christine and I were smoking crack. I was also snorting coke. We were the most depressed people around. No Christian person can run from Jesus and be happy, because deep down inside, you know that you are running from God's grace. But you do not think that Jesus will ever want you back; Satan has a strong hold on your life and will make you think it's too late to go back to Christ.

There were times I would be so messed up on drugs I would not remember how I got home. Thank God I did not kill myself or someone else. I would go on drug missions, trying to score more to smoke, and I would talk to people I did not know. There in the drug world, I was just lucky I only got scammed for money.

Sometimes I almost got killed or beaten up on bad drug deals. It was plain stupid. Give Satan a chance, and he would love to take you out of this life. I thank Jesus for watching over me during those dark days.

Nobody wanted to do drugs with me, because I would be a downer and say, "Why are we doing drugs? This will mess up our life. I know Jesus does not want us on these things." The conviction of the Holy Spirit was totally working on me. My dear readers, you do not realize that Jesus will never give up on you. If you still have breath to breathe, you still have hope. If you have an addiction, Jesus Christ can set you free from it.

After a lot of years, I was really addicted to drunkenness and drug use. I could not go without drinking for a day or without drugs on the weekend. The devil had a strong hold on me, and until I was willing to totally surrender to God, I would not be set free.

After Christine's mother died right at my home a day before my birthday in March, Jesus worked on Christine about surrendering her life to him. She said she asked Jesus to forgive her for all her sins and to come into her heart so she could live for him. I was totally shocked that Jesus opened her eyes before me. I was ready to change; the Spirit of God spoke to my heart and said, *You need to stop running from me. She will need your help in the faith to overcome the devil's schemes.*

So one day, while I was driving for a different truck company, I started to pray out loud to God. At first, the devil had me thinking, *There's no way he would set me free from my habits, because I knew better but still did them.* But what it was, was that Jesus wanted me to really want to change my life 100 percent, not make a partial surrender to him. My dear reader, for Jesus to come into your life, you cannot give up some of your sins and hang on to others. It is a total surrender of your life.

As I was screaming out to Jesus to help me stop doing drugs and liquor, after a couple of minutes, something strange happened. I could smell freshly cooked crack and pure Jack Daniel's in my truck. I cried out, "Jesus, how is smelling freshly cooked crack and liquor going to help me quit my drug use?" He then spoke to my mind and said, *My son, this is all the drugs in your body cleared out. I have purged from your bloodstream and body all traces of drug use, so now you will not crave any of them again.*

Guess what? Currently, in my life of drugs and liquor, I have been free since 2003 until the present. I have not wanted it or missed it at all. Do not think that the devil did not try to get me to slip; there were times in the past that Satan would send people my way to offer me free drugs or liquor. But I stood firm. I did not want it. It was a waste of my time.

CHAPTER 40

Miscellaneous Miracles

There was one day that I was driving a semi and a trailer on a highway going to New Berlin, Wisconsin. It was snowing on the freeway. Before I knew it, my trailer started to jackknife, and I started to lose control of the rig. I cried out, "Jesus, help me!" At that split second, God corrected my semi and trailer. It was as if I never lost control, and I had good driving for the rest of the day. Thank God for protecting me that day. This one verse is my favorite because it applies to every one of our lives in Christ.

> We know that all things work together for good for those who love God, for those who are called according to his purpose. (Romans 8:28)

I have learned throughout my life that Jesus is always teaching me things about him and how I can relate my life to him. He is good at showing us things in our life that need to be adjusted or changed to become more Christlike.

It took me a long time to realize that I was doing things for selfish reasons at times. It is a mistake to think God owes us anything. We all owe him our lives for what he did on the cross. He took away our eternal death sentence at Calvary for all the sins we ever committed.

Until about 2006, I tried to get a good-paying job, but no matter how hard I tried, I seemed to always get subpar jobs and barely made enough money to pay my bills. I thought God did not want me to have too much income so I would have to always rely on him only to provide my every need. This is true, of course, but that was not the reason Jesus never gave me a high-paying job. Jesus said in his Word, "How can a man be trusted with great riches if he's not faithful in the least?" This was when God tested my faith and my motives.

For years, I tried to get a job at FedEx or UPS. The doors never opened. After I recommitted my life to Jesus, I was working for Quicksilver as a truck driver. I was there, averaging about $9 an hour. There was a day that I talked to another driver who was very new, and I thought that he knew extraordinarily little compared to me about the freight industry. Also, he was an unsaved person. So my thinking was, *I should be paid more than this man because I am Christ's child.* Jesus had to show me that my thinking was all wrong.

The first thing God did was get this man a great job in this other company, driving a truck. I was already experienced and had been driving for many years, and here he got this great-paying job with little driving skills. So I was a little jealous that he got this job and not me.

One day, I was praying to Jesus about how I could be more faithful to him and be a better servant and good soul winner. Currently, I was doing prison ministry at the Racine jail. While I was praying, Jesus brought the fellow worker to my mind who got the good job instead of me. Suddenly, I had a negative feeling about this man and his good fortune. Then Jesus spoke to my heart (mind), *Why are you mad about this person?*

I knew about this time that God was going to show me a life lesson. I said, "Jesus, why did you never get me a good-paying job? But this unbeliever comes along, and you give him a good job."

Then it was like a light went on in my soul. My motives and attitude were all wrong. I said, "Jesus, you said we need to pray for others and love our enemy. You love this man also, so who am I to complain about things you do in his life? Jesus, please forgive me for that bad way of thinking." Jesus died for all my sins, past, present, and future. He showed me that I was always forgiven, and I was glad I learned this life lesson.

From that day forward, I prayed for that man, and I was grateful for that job at Quicksilver. I never complained about my money problems again. I knew that God was in control; I had nothing to worry about anymore. My life was going to have some major changes in the coming years ahead.

God put it in my heart one day, while I was reading the newspaper, that a place called AmeriGas was looking for drivers. I felt God was leading me there. Also, the starting pay was $13 per hour, compared to the $9 per hour average at Quicksilver. I prayed, *Lord, if you want me to leave Quicksilver, have them call me and give me an interview for the job.*

As it went, I got to the company to fill out an application. I turned in the filled-out application, and the manager came out to interview me. Just like the Lord placed in my heart that I was getting the new job, the Lord was pleased that I was content with my old job and that I was obedient to his leading to take this new job. Of course, $13 per hour would help me with my financial needs at the time. Little did I know that Jesus had plans that were unexpected in the following months ahead.

I was happy at this time, working with a propane company and delivering propane gas to different locations while driving a bobtail to fill low-propane tanks. My wife, of course, was a little concerned about me working what could be an extremely dangerous job. Propane is a highly combustible and very flammable gas. I guess I should never have told her about the man at my job who got some majors burns on his body from a propane accident at the filling station at work.

Getting back to the Lord's involvement in a major blessing for me and my wife's benefit, this blessing was twofold. One was that God was pleased I stopped thinking I needed more income to live on, because Jesus was the Provider of my needs. The other thing in my life would come in the form of a test of my faith, to leave a job on his leading.

I finished my probationary period, and with the overtime, I was making good money. God also had me involved in prison ministry; I had time off for weekends, so I could do both prison ministry and church. One day, when I went to work, my manager called me to her office to tell me about some crazy changes for my new job hours and days. Now when I took the job, I was told it was Monday through Friday. My manager said that since I was low on the totem pole, I would have to work weekends and different hours. I asked what hours, and what she told me floored me. The hours would make it an impossibility for me to go to church or do the prison ministry. I know the Lord blessed me, in that a lot of inmates were giving their lives to God at the Racine jail. I tried to see if I could have off time at least for church and the jail ministering time, but my manager would not budge on the work hours. I said, "I might have to resign, because I need to go to church and I cannot give up my jail ministry." This was on Friday. I had to decide before Monday whether to work those new hours.

I prayed extremely hard that weekend. "Jesus, I do not want to give up church or the jail ministry. What should I do?" These were some of the things I prayed about. I got the Sunday paper that day, and as I got to the employment section, I said, "Jesus, there are a lot of truck driving jobs listed. So as I read through the ads, have the job you want me to take jump out at me, and I will call them. Of course, Jesus, could you help me get at least $13 an hour, please? But not mine, but your will be done."

As I was going through the ads, this one job jumped right out at me. It was called Double J Transport. It was looking for a full-time truck driver, and it would be Monday through Friday. Also, I would have time off for church and my jail ministry. Before I called, I prayed out loud, saying, "Jesus, if this is the job you want me to take, have them hire me over the phone." The reason I said this was that I noticed that the job location was in Jackson, Wisconsin. That would be far away from Milwaukee, Wisconsin. That was forty miles one way to work daily; that would be awfully expensive for gas in a week.

So I called this employer on the phone, and the man who did the hiring answered the phone. I asked about the job and what it would be and the basic job duties daily and the starting pay. The pay floored me. It was $13 per hour and incentive pay. This was a 30% commission, so that I would never make less than $13 per hour on my percentage of work. Then I mumbled a little prayer. "Well, Jesus, if this is the job, have me get hired over the phone."

After the man explained the job to me, I told him about all the work experience I had. Again, the Lord floored me, because the employer hired me right over the phone—no live interview, no application to fill out. I just had to come at that time to fill out the paperwork for employment. Again, I was saying to the Lord as I drove, "Jesus, I hope I do not have to drive far from home to work daily."

The man said, "You will work at the company called Watkins Motor Lines as a contractor and truck driver." It was located on Thirteenth Street in Milwaukee, between College Avenue and Rawson Avenue. This place would have my truck parked there daily. Praise God, the job was only about seven miles from home. There would be no long drive to work daily. As you can tell, Jesus Christ really blessed me at that point, so I figured this was my blessing for putting his will first in my life.

Just as a reminder, all my truck-driving days, I tried to get a job working for UPS or FedEx, and no doors ever opened when I tried. I found out that God has a divine plan for all his children, but only on his timetable. Little did I know that Jesus was not done blessing my wife and I with a higher purpose in mind and people to meet to help guide them to Christ.

I had been working for about a little over a month at Watkins, and a rumor was going around the drivers that FedEx was going to buy out Watkins's motor line. I was only a contractor for Watkins, so if they sold their company to FedEx, what would happen to the private contracted helpers who did not work directly with Watkins? This, of course, gave the devil a field day in my mind, saying things like *Now what? You will not have a job. See, you should have stayed at AmeriGas. God's not blessing you. You should have not quit your other job.* With all this and more negative thoughts going through my mind, Jesus had me think about Job's life and how even if Satan tries to do things to you and your life, he can only do what God allows him to. The great thing is, at the end of Job's story, he had a happy, blessed life and double what he started with. So I said to the demons that were tormenting my thoughts, *Devil, Jesus loves me, and everything will work out for my good in my life because Jesus is in charge. Nothing can happen without his permission in my life.*

CHAPTER 41

Truck Driving Miracles

While I went to work daily at Watkins, I tried not to think about what would happen if FedEx did buy out Watkins. About two weeks went by without us private contractors knowing if we would even have a job anymore. I went home one day after my driving shift was over, and my wife said, "Rick, you got a letter from FedEx."

At first, when I heard this, I was thinking, *Well, this is it. I might not have a job anymore.* I thought this because my boss had told me that if Watkins sells, I could not work for him anymore. So I prayed, *Jesus, whatever happens from here on, I know you will always provide for my needs according to your riches and glory.*

Guess what? Jesus was still not done blessing my life, because this was not a termination letter. It was a job offer and a job upgrade. The letter floored me. It said, "We would like to hire you at $19.85 per hour and train you as you work for us to learn how to drive a semi daily." Yes, I had a class B driver's license. After having training, while getting paid, I would have a class A driver's license. I praised God for this job upgrade and a change of my job skills. This opened doors for me and my wife to have a job until I retired from truck driving, with a good benefit to boot.

In over fifteen years, Jesus has really blessed me here at FedEx Freight. I had to learn a lot of things here. It was hard at times, but God has come through in everything I've faced since then. I have been a truly blessed man. I thank Jesus Christ and God the Father for everything he has done in my life to this day and onward.

My dear reader, Jesus can and will change your life if you surrender your will and life to him today. You need to come clean with God and admit that you are a lost sinner and have need for a Savior in your life. Let Jesus help you from this day forward. Believe that he died for your sins and that he rose again from the dead to save you and raise your soul from the dead and give you a new spirit within you today. Ask him to wash away your sins with his blood and to fill you with his Holy Spirit today.

At the end of my life story, I will give you places to contact for furthering your growth in Christ. Read your Bible daily and pray to God for understanding of his Word. Find a Bible-believing church that teaches you that Jesus is the Lord and that the whole Bible is inspired by God. My favorite verses are about the new birth.

> Jesus answered him, "Most certainly, I tell you, unless one is born anew, he can't see God's Kingdom." Nicodemus said to him, "How can a man be born when he is old? Can he enter a second time into his mother's womb, and be born?" Jesus answered, "Most certainly I tell you, unless one is born of water and spirit, he can't enter into God's Kingdom. That which is born of the flesh is flesh. That which is born of the Spirit is spirit. Don't marvel that I said to you, 'You must be born anew.' The wind blows where it wants to, and you hear its sound, but don't know where it comes from and where it is going. So is everyone who is born of the Spirit." (John 3:3–8)

CHAPTER 42

Recent Miracles

First, every day that I get up in the morning with Jesus Christ in my life is a blessing and a miracle. As a driver, I have been helped by God countless times in getting out of some close calls with bad drivers around me daily. He helped me be the most proficient driver also. Do not get me wrong, I am not perfect; I made some mistakes as a driver.

One day, I was finishing up my driving duties, and on the way home, I had a minor fender bender on the job. I did not want any more accidents on my record. I prayed, "Jesus, please help me be a better and safer driver from this day forward. Also, any more accidents might hurt my driving record, so keep me out of dangerous driving situations."

It was not but a couple of days after my work-related incident that God prevented me from having another freak accident. This one day, I was driving with a new box trailer and a new semi-tractor with exceptionally low mileage on it. My shift was about over, and I was starting to do my pickup for work. I was driving down Highway 18 in Wisconsin. The speed limit was 55 in this stretch of the county where I was driving.

Just as I was turning on Highway 18, my tractor lights started to tell me that my tractor was having a malfunction. The engine was starting to lose power, so I pulled over onto the shoulder of the highway. It died out. I tried to start up the new tractor, and it would do nothing. It was turned off completely—no clicks, no dash lights, nothing weird. About five minutes went by. I said, "Jesus, help me get the truck started, please."

About a minute passed, and the Lord spoke to me and said, *Start the truck. It's safe to drive now.*

So I turned the ignition key to start the engine, and it fired right up as if nothing was wrong with the engine. I thanked Jesus for his help and pulled out safely from the shoulder. As I was getting the rig up to the speed limit, I was about a mile down the road when, out of nowhere, a buck ran right in front of my semi and crossed to the other side of the road. I just missed hitting the deer.

If I had been on that patch of highway any earlier, I would have had another accident involving a deer on my driving record. I believe it was God who stalled my truck for enough time so that the deer that was running from someplace would get to that part of the highway before I got there, helping me avoid hitting the deer. Jesus has helped me since then to have a good driving record until the present time.

It is a shocker that my last written miracles that Jesus did were in recent times, 2020 through 2021. This happened twice within a year's time. The first time, I went to see a doctor at the hospital because I had noticed that when I would try to urinate in the bathroom, extraordinarily little dribbles, or none at all, would come out. It was really frustrating to have to go to the bathroom fifteen plus times and never get much out. It was time to get checked out by a doctor. They ran all kinds of tests and said they could not figure out why I could not pee at all or would pee extraordinarily little. After hours of testing, they said, "Go home and think about going under the knife to find out more ways to help you urinate." Or I would have to run a special snake tool up my male tubing, which no male would wish to have to endure.

As I was getting ready to leave the hospital, I felt an urge again to empty my bladder. I walked up to the urinal and prayed, *Jesus, please help me pee again. I do not want to go for any surgery so that I can pee again.* So I relaxed the muscle down there, and it started out very weak at first. I whispered again, "Help me, Jesus," and just like that, I instantly felt something solid come out of my private. Then a solid stream came out. I was urinating normally now. I had to see what came out of my tubing, and a bluish-black chunk was resting just inside the urinal. It was excessively big. I was shocked that something the size of a kidney stone had come out, and I had felt no pain when it came out. I looked it up online to determine what the object was.

About six months later, my bladder was starting to act up again. I prayed, *Jesus, something sharp is working its way out. Please help it come out without really bad pain.* About two weeks later, I was relieving myself, and something solid came out again. It was a noticeably big calcium stone with a pointed edge that came out, but truly little pain came with the exit of the stone from my body. I praised God for healing my body so that I could pee normally again.

I thank God that you found time to read this true story of the things Christ Jesus and God the Father have done throughout my life. As you can tell, it is a miracle that I am even still alive today after most of the things I went through in my lifetime. There were a lot of other things I could have shared with you all; I just did not want to make the book too long. I just want all my readers to know that Jesus Christ is very much alive today, as he was during the time the Bible was completely written down for us to read. So please pray and ask Jesus to save and help you today. Remember, he died for all the sins you have committed in your life. No one will be turned away from God today.

In closing, think about lasting life. God did not go to all the trouble of sending his Son merely to point an accusing finger and tell the world how bad it was. He came to save you from your lost condition. If you are not his son or daughter today, pray right now and ask him into your heart and life today. My dear reader, if you are backslidden, Jesus still loves you. No amount of sin will keep him from setting you free still. We need to comprehend he paid for all our sins committed—past, present, and future ones. The Word of God says where sin did abound, God's grace did much more abound.

When I look back at how many times I slipped up and fell from God's grace, he, like a good shepherd leave the ninety-nine faithful sheep, came after me each time and brought me back to his home. One day in prayer, God in love rebuked me for my blindness of his grace in my life. I said, "Lord, I am so embarrassed that after all these miracles in my life, I walk away at times." Then he reminds me of a prayer I made when I was twelve years old. Jesus asked me, "What was one of the things I said to you before I left you there with girls that pray with you?" Then a light went on in my thoughts. He said to me, "My son, someday I will take you home to be with me in heaven. So, my child, why would I change my mind? I will always love you."

So, my friends, it's never too late to surrender your will to his will for your life.

My closing thought is that during this COVID-19 outbreak, I give thanks to Christ Jesus my Lord and God the Father. Our Savior has kept me positive during this time.

In this story, I told you about how Jesus pulled up my hands at least three times before he filled me completely with his Holy Spirit. One day, while I was praying in church, I asked God in prayer many times for him to pull my hands up toward heaven, and for a while, there was no response to that request. The reason I wanted God to pull up my hands again was that the joy and peace and love I felt was out of this world.

This one day in church, Jesus talked to me in the still, small voice and said, *I will do it one more time, my child.*

I was overly excited about this and replied, "When, Lord, will you do this?"

His response was *The next time your hands go up by themselves is when I take you home with me.*

Praise God, my friends. That could be the rapture of the church body or when Jesus takes me from this life to the hereafter. To all believers, take comfort in this. Jesus will take us home someday. Yes, it is the blessed hope of all his saints.

If you need to contact me for anything, speaking engagements to share my testimonies, or book signings, let me know. Also please let me know if you gave your life to Jesus Christ because of my story. Email fpaetzke@yahoo.com or write to Chaplain Rick Paetzke 10550 W Cortez Circle APT 4 Franklin WI 53132.

Yours in Christ,
Chaplain Rick Paetzke

Then we which are alive and remain shall be caught up together with them in the clouds, to meet the Lord in the air: and so, shall we ever be with the Lord. (1 Thessalonians 4:17 KJV)

If you accepted Jesus as Lord of your life, you need to find a church that teaches the new birth experience. Remember, just walk by faith. Lord bless you, my dear readers.

ABOUT THE AUTHOR

Chaplain Rick Paetzke is currently living in Franklin, Wisconsin, with his beloved wife and precocious granddaughter, Analisa. He is still working and spends his spare time with his family. He enjoys fishing with his son Kevin at any given opportunity during the long summer months. He also enjoys visiting his daughter when she's able to make the journey from Florida. He is readily available to do the Lord's work at any given chance. He likes to spend time reading and enjoys eating out at the local George Webb's for breakfast on Saturday mornings and vacationing with family up north.

One of the things he loves most is going to jails and other places to teach others about the grace of God and to help people who were bound by drugs and alcohol because Jesus set him free from both. Yes, living free from addiction is a wonderful life to live in the world today, and he hopes that we give Jesus our heart today. He gets great joy today when he shares his life story with people he has never met before, to see their faces shine with shock or amazement at knowing what Jesus did for him and what he can do for them. He believes he needs to comfort others with the love of God today.

CPSIA information can be obtained
at www.ICGtesting.com
Printed in the USA
JSHW051149040922
29959JS00001B/4